Understanding Practical English

edited by

Justin Hiraga · Jeehye Pak

우용출판사
1997
www.choolpansa.com

Justin Hiraga

Assistant Professor at Woosuk University- Department of Distribution & Trade, Korea

B.S. Landscape Architecture, University of California, Davis, CA, U.S.A.
M.S. (Management), Graduate School of Business, Sungkyunkwan University, Seoul, Korea
Doctoral student, Dept. of International Trade, Graduate School, Sungkyunkwan University
TEFL & Business TEFL Certified
Former Landscape Architect for the Central Park Conservancy, NY

Jeehye Pak

Director of Korea Office, Eye Square GmbH

B.A. Psychology, University of North Texas, TX, U.S.A.
Research Student, Department of Marine Policy and Culture, Tokyo University of Marine Science and Technology, Japan
Former Research Consultant, Global Research Division for Hankook Research, Seoul
Former Case Manager for the New York Asian Women's Center, U.S.A

Understanding Practical English

2011년 08월 23일 초판 1쇄 인쇄
2011년 08월 31일 초판 1쇄 발행

저자 / Justin Hiraga · Jeehye Park
발행인 / 고우용
발행처 / 우용출판사
등록일 / 1997년 11월 25일
출판등록 / 제 313-1997-139호
주소 / 서울특별시 마포구 망원1동 338-53
전화번호 / 02)324-6577
팩시밀리 / 02)324-6177

정가 / 17,000원

ISBN / 978-89-6249-060-2

Understanding Practical English / Preface

English has become the global language and as a result, thousands upon thousands of English instruction books have flooded the bookstores. Through my years of teaching English to non-native speakers, I have gone through my fair share of textbooks. Each book has some merits, yet failed in one crucial aspect. These books lacked the practicality and flexibility that is necessary to learn and more importantly, master English as a language.

Instead of learning canned phrases or formulaic dialogues, it is important to learn a variety of techniques and ways to express yourself in English. Thus, Practical English fulfills this gap. It allows the student to learn a variety of expressions in order to give students the freedom to choose how to express themselves based on their own circumstances and personalities.

In order to continue English education to the next level, this book was based off of native speakers' and Korean teachers' contemporary educational techniques to study Practical English in many different channels. Hence, this book has strategically concentrated on Vocabulary building, Dialogue practice, Composition, and Reading skills, so that English can be practiced and associated with various settings.

Included as well, is an Appendix to introduce Business English as a jump-start into your careers. It will introduce you to key concepts and words, as well as provide relevant activities that encourage you to start thinking in English.

My hope is that this book will break down your fears of learning English and allow you to adapt the English language to your own personality. Practical English is a first step in creating an English voice for you to speak up and be heard.

Justin Hiraga
July 15, 2011

Contents

HELLO

my name is

INTRODUCTION

1. Common Words, Idioms and Expressions 1

to introduce
to address
informality
to ignore
host / hostess
to phrase
leave-taking / greeting
to embrace
to bow
formal / informal
etiquette

for a while
to shake hands
to drop by
to be conscious of
in spite of
to be followed
for instance / example
to stand up
to be sure
to talk about

2. Common Words, Idioms and Expressions 2

How do you do?
I'm very pleased to meet you.

I'm very happy to meet you.
The pleasure is mine.

It's very kind of you to say so.

Come and see us sometime.
Drop by my house sometime.

Allow me to introduce to you my friend, Mr. Smith.

DIALOGUE

Read the Text:

1. A: Let me introduce myself to you.
   My name is Tom Smith.
   B: How do you do?
   A: I'm glad to meet you.
   B: May I have your card?
   A: Sure. Here you are.
   B: Thanks a lot.
   A: How do I address you?
   B: Kim. What was your name again, please?
   A: Tom Smith. It was nice meeting you.

2. A: Mary, I'd like to introduce you to my good friend, John Brooks. John, this is Mary Harrington.
   B: How do you do?
   C: How do you do, Miss Harrington?
   A: You'll probably be seeing a lot of Mary for the next week or so, John. She's going to be staying with us for a while.
   C: I'm happy to hear that. I hope you'll enjoy your stay here.
   B: Oh, I'm sure I will. Everyone has been so kind to me.

Exercise A: Restate your part of the conversation from the text.

1. Let me introduce myself to you. My name is Tom Smith.
2. May I have your card?
3. How do I address you?
4. How do you do?
5. I'm happy to hear that. I hope you'll enjoy your stay here.

Exercise B: Fill in the blanks.

1. May I introduce (   )? I'm John Hampton.
2. When you are being introduced, listen carefully to (   ) name.
3. Mr. President, (   ) me to present my sister, Mrs. Smith.
4. Drop (   ) my house sometime.
5. Boys and men usually shake (   ) upon being introduced.

COMPOSITION

Read the Text:

In America or England, however, a women sometimes extends her hand to a man or to another woman, but this is not necessary. She does not have to stand up in introductions, either. When she rises, she does so only to show special respect to another person for his age or position. Both Americans and Englishmen are very friendly, but their greetings and leave-takings are often short and informal. When two friends meet or when they say good-bye, they sometimes shake hands, and sometimes do not. They do not embrace. They do not bow.

Excercise A: Answer the questions 1 to 5 in complete sentences.

1. What is this story about?
2. To whom does a woman sometimes extend her hand?
3. What doesn't she have to do in introductions?
4. Are Englishmen's leave-takings often long and informal?
5. When do they sometimes shake hands?

Exercise B: Make sentences following the example.

Ex: woman / extends / another

A women sometimes extends her hand to a man or to another woman.

1. she / stand / introduction
2. she / show / respect
3. American / Englishman / friendly
4. their greetings / leave-takings / informal
5. they / sometimes / hands

READING

Read the Text:

Few rules of etiquette are easier to learn, and few are more often broken, than the simple rules for making and accepting introductions. As with invitations, introduction may be formal or very informal, or halfway between, but in any case they should make both parties to the introduction comfortable and at ease. For formal introductions there are set rules: always introduce men to women, "Mrs. Smith, may I introduce (or present) Mr. Jones?"

This rule is reversed if the man is a very importance person, for example, the President of the United States, or a minister, or a distinguished visitor. You would then say, "Mr. President, permit me to present Mrs. Thomas Smith." In all cases if you are doing the introducing, be sure that you pronounce the names clearly and distinctly, and if you are one of those being introduced be sure to catch the name and remember it. Often it is a matter if further courtesy if you identify the individuals being introduced by more than just their names. For instance, you might like to say, "Mr. President, permit me to present my sister, Mrs. Tomas Smith, from Cleveland." Immediately, the newly introduced people will have something to talk about. They can talk about Cleveland!

Exercise A: Indicate whether each of the following statements is true or false by writing the letter T or F in the space provided.

— 1. As with invitations, introductions may be formal or very informal, or halfway between.

— 2. For formal introductions there are set rules: always introduce women to men.

— 3. In all cases, if you are doing the introducing, be sure that you pronounce the names clearly and distinctly.

— 4. If you are one of those being introduced, be sure to catch the name and remember it.

— 5. Immediately, the newly introduced people will have something to talk about.

Exercise B: How do you introduce two people whom you know, but who do not know each other?

Lesson 2

GREETING

1. Useful Words and Idioms

greeting / salutation
mental / physical
to introduce
customary
to lift
to rub
to snap
health
to feel well
What's the matter with you?
to catch cold
to be expected to
to remove one's hat
on parting
to show friendly concern
to touch the brim

2. Common Expressions

Hi.
Hello.
Good morning / afternoon / evening.
Good-bye.

How are you doing?
How is it going?
What's new?
What's up?

Good / nice to see you again.

Nothing in particular.
Not much.
So, so.

I'm all right. / O. K.

So far, so good / difficult.

DIALOGUE

Read the Text:

1. A: Hi! Bob. How are you?
   B: Fine, thanks. And you?
   A: Very well, thank you.
   B: Where are you headed?
   A: I'm on my way to my business.
   B: How's your business?
   A: The same as ever. Give my regard to your folks.
   B: Thanks. I'll be seeing you. (So long.)

2. A: How's it going, Mike?
   B: All right. What are you going to do tomorrow?
   A: I don't have any plans. Why?
   B: I'm going to see the soccer game.
   Do you want to go with me?
   A: OK. I'll be glad to. See you tomorrow, John.
   B: Good night, Mike.

Exercise A: Restate your part of the conversation from the text.

1. Hi! Bob. How are you?
2. Where are you headed?
3. How's your business?
4. Good evening, Mike.
5. Do you want to go with me?

Exercise B: Fill in the blanks.

1. How's ( )?
2. How's it ( )?
3. Isn't ( ) a wonderful day?
4. Fine, ( ), and how are you?
5. I'm going back ( ) good.

COMPOSITION

Read the Text:

If two men who haven't seen each other for a long time meet, they may stop and shake hands.

It is polite for a man when meeting a woman to remove his hat. It is not necessary, however, for him to completely remove his hat from his head — he may merely touch the brim and slightly nod his head. In America, a man does not remove his hat when he meets another man.

A man is expected to rise when a woman or an elderly person enters the room. In small towns people usually speak to each other when they pass on the street — whether they have been introduced or not. This is not done in larger towns.

Exercise A: Answer the questions 1 to 5 in complete sentences.

1. If two men who haven't seen each other for a long time meet, what may they do?
2. Is it polite for a man when meeting a woman to remove his hat?
3. In America, does a man remove his hat when he meets another man?
4. What is a man expected to do when a woman enters the room?
5. In small towns do people usually speak to each other when they pass on the street?

Exercise B: Make sentences following the example.

Ex: they / stop / shake
They may stop and shake hands.

1. polite / meeting / remove
2. necessary / however / his head
3. merely / brim / slightly
4. expected / elderly / enters
5. small / usually / pass on

READING

Read the Text:

SALUTATION, a gesture of recognition or greeting exchanged when people meet. The word is derived from the Latin salus, meaning health or safety, and a spoken salutation in most languages is generally meant to convey good wishes, even though expressions like "How do you do" have lost their original meanings and have become purely formal. "Good-bye" is a contraction of "God be with you." The Arab greeting is "Peace be with you," and the conventional reply is, "And with you also."

There are many gestures of greeting that are not spoken. Every group of people sharing a common culture has its own customary forms of salutation. The Ainus rub their palms together, some Negro peoples snap or crack their fingers ceremoniously, and the Eskimos sometimes rub noses in greeting each other. Hugging and kissing as forms of salutation, even between strangers, have been customary in some countries at various times.

The custom of shaking hands is fairly widespread in the Western nations. It probably had its origin in the primitive way of lifting the empty right hand to show that no harm was intended. Clasping hands was a gesture of trust, because the right hand was the one that would normally hold a weapon. Eventually shaking hands came to mean a seal of acceptance on a bargain or agreement.

Exercise A: Indicate whether each of following statements is true or false by writing the letter T or F in the space provided.

— 1. Salutation, a gesture of recognition or greeting exchanged when people meet.

— 2. "Good-bye" is a contraction of "How do you do?"

— 3. Some Negro peoples rub noses in greeting each other.

— 4. Hugging and kissing as forms of salutation have been customary in Korea at various times.

— 5. Clasping hands was a gesture of trust, because the right hand was the one that would normally hold a weapon.

Exercise B: If you meet someone you haven't seen for a long time, what would you do?

Lesson 3

WEATHER

1. Useful Words and Idioms

weather / climate
freezing
season
weather report
temperature
Fahrenheit
Centigrade
weather bureau
to shovel
to one's surprise
to get in
to look like
to save one's life
to have in common with
to be measured in
to clear up
a number of
to stay home
to get angry

2. Common Expressions

It is fine / fair / sunny / favorable / good / clear.

splendid / charming / beautiful / glorious / lovely.
calm / mild / genial / serene.
foul / bad / nasty / ugly / rainy / wretched / beastly.
fickle / changeable / unsettled.
seasonable / unseasonable.
gloomy / oppressive.
perfect / ideal.
threatening.

warm / hot / cool / cold / humid / dry.

windy / sunny / cloudy / rainy / snowy.

DIALOGUE

Read the Text :

1. A: Let's get in. I'm freezing.
   B: Yes, the wind feels like a knife.
   A: The radio says it'll snow tomorrow.
   B: You can never tell whether it will rain or snow.
   A: Winter is colder here than in my country.
2. A: What's the climate like in your country?
   B: It's very pleasant.
   A: Which season do you like best?
   A: I like fall best.
   B: Why?
   A: Because it's warm and the scenery is very beautiful.
3. A: I wonder what the weather is going to be like.
   B: The newspaper says it's going to be fair and sunny.
   A: Let's listen to the weather report on the radio.
   B: That's a good idea.

Exercise A: Restate your part of the conversation from the test.

1. Let's get in. I'm freezing.
2. The radio says it'll snow tomorrow.
3. What's the climate like in your country?
4. Which season do you like best?
5. Why do you like fall best?

Exercise B: Fill in the blanks.

1. I hope the rain lets ( ) by noon, dont' you?
2. Haven't we been ( ) wonderful weather?
3. We sure do need a rain, ( ) we?
4. Looks ( ) it might snow.
5. I do hope we'll ( ) nice weather for our picnic tomorrow afternoon.

COMPOSITION

Read the Text:

In America almost every conversation begins with a comment about the weather. People talk about the weather when they don't know what else to say, or when they have very little in common with the person to whom they are talking.

There is a great variety of temperature change between Northern and Southern America. The North is very cold in the winter, while the South has much warmer winters with no snow.

In America there is no season in which there is especially heavy rains as in Korea in the months of June and July. The South has more rain while the West has very little rain.

The temperature in America is measured in Fahrenheit degrees instead of Centigrade degrees. January is normally the coldest month, and June is the warmest.

Exercise A: Answer the questions 1. to 5 in complete sentences.

1. What do people talk about when they don't know what else to say?
2. How is the weather between Northen and Southern America?
3. Where is it very cold in the winter?
4. How many seasons are there in Korea?
5. What is normally the coldest month in America?

Exercise B: Make sentences following the example.

Ex: America / conversation / the weather
In America almost every conversation begins with a comment about the weather.

1. they / common / talking
2. while / South / warmer
3. America / no season / rains
4. South / while / little
5. temperature / measured / Fahrenheit

READING

Read the Text:

It was winter and the weather was very bad. It snowed hard and many people stayed home. They didn't even go to work.

The Robinsons also stayed home for a few days. The children didn't go to school and Mr. Robinson didn't go to work.

One morning the weather cleared up and Mr. Robinson thought, "It's time to go to work!" He went to the backyard to check his car in the garage. The driveway, however, was covered with snow. Mr. Robinson went back into the house and called a man to come and shovel the snow. A half hour later the man came and Mr. Robinson gave him instructions. He said to the man, "I want you to clear the driveway, but don't shovel any snow on the left because it might ruin Mrs. Robinson's vegetable garden. And don't put any snow on the right side because it might ruin our lawn. And of course don't throw any snow in the street because the neighbors will get very angry." Then Mr. Robinson went back into the house and left the man to shovel the snow.

An hour later, the man came into the house and said, "The driveway is cleared." Mr. Robinson paid him and the man left. Mr. Robinson then looked out of the window, and sure enough, the driveway was cleared. There was no snow on the right side and there was none in the garden or tn the street. He was very pleased. He then put on his coat and boots and went out to the garage. He open the garage door and to his surprise he saw the garage filled to the top with the snow from the driveway, and somewhere under it all was his car!

Exercise A: Indicate whether each of the following statements is true or false by writing the letter T or F in the space provided.

— 1. The winter snowed hard and many people stayed home. They didn't even go to work.

— 2. One morning Mr Robinson went to the backyard to check his car.

— 3. Mr. Robinson went back into the house and called a man to come and shovel the snow.
— 4. The next day, the man came said, "The driveway is cleared."
— 5. Mr. Robinson opened the garage door and to his surprise saw it cleared.

Exercise B: Give a brief account of the weather in your country.

CUSTOM

1. Useful Words and Idioms

teen-ager
to be different from
oriental / occidental
on public
appointment
impression
pet
magic
proverb
hemisphere
cumbersome
to bring up
to avoid
to get out of
to be on time
to ask for
all the time
to get along
to be necessary to
to be bound to
to point out

2. Common Expressions

some customary opening remarks when you first arrive:

Come in.
Come in please.
May I have your coat?
Just make your at home.
Go right into other room, please.
Won't you please sit down?

some customary remarks when leaving:

I really must be going.
It's getting late.
I'm going to have to leave now.
Oh, my! Look time it is. I must be leaving.
I've got to go home. I have to get up early in the morning.

DIALOGUE

Read the Text:

1. A: Do you have dating in your country?
   B: I think there is some dating in my country.
   A: What's your impression of dating?
   B: It seems rather extreme to see young teen-agers going out on dates.
   A: The culture is different here, and children are brought up with these ideas.
   B: Yes. What is right in one country is often wrong in another.
   A: So, it is safe to remember that "In Rome do as the Romans do."
   B: By doing so, everybody cam avoid making a mistake in a foreign country.
2. A: Customs are different in every country.
   B: But they are not too different between Western countries.
   A: That's right
   B: But the customs of an Oriental country are quite different from those of a Western country.
   A: For example, it is taboo in America to eat with your mouth open.
   B: Yes, it is true. Is it the same in Korea?
   A: I would say no.

Exercise A: Restate your part of the conversation from the text.

1. Do you have dating in your country?
2. What's your impression of dating?
3. Customs are same in every country.
4. Are customs too different between Western countries?
5. Is it taboo in America to eat with your mouth open?

Exercise B: Fill in the blanks.

1. A man should (   ) whenever a woman enters the room.
2. Men also (   ) packages for older people.
3. A man should (   ) his hat when entering any office.
4. A woman does not (   ) while introduced to a man.
5. If a woman drops something, a man should (   ) it up for her.

COMPOSITION

Read the Text:

There are some things you shouldn't do. Don't tell the truth when people ask "How are you?" They only expect the answer to be "Fine." Never ask people their age — especially women! Everyone wants to be young. Don't tell heavy people they are fat. Tell them they are losing weight. Everyone here is diet — conscious and wants to be thin. Don't be late for appointments! When someone says six o'clock, be sure to be there by six. Americans respect time and expect every one to be "on time."

Exercise A: Answer the questions 1 to 5 in complete sentences.

1. Do they only expect the answer to be "Fine" when people ask "How are you?"
2. Why shouldn't you ask women their age?
3. Why shouldn't you tell people they are fat?
4. Why is it important to be on time?
5. What time should you arrive for a six o'clock appointment?

Exercise B: Make sentences following the example.

Ex: there / some things / shouldn't
There are some things you shouldn't do.

1. truth / ask / how are you
2. never / their age / women
3. tell / they / fat
4. says / sure / by six
5. America / expect / on time

READING

Read the Text:

"When in Rome, do as the Romans do." So goes an old English proverb. This is generally good advice for a person in a strange country. In order to follow it, it is necessary to know what the Romans do and, more important, what their attitudes and beliefs are.

Every society has its own peculiar customs and ways of acting. The United States contains over 180 million people. They have a wide variety of national backgrounds, so there are bound to be regional and temperamental differences. The reader should remember that when he or she reads that Americans do this or that or think this or that, not all Americans do think this particular thing or if they do today, they may not tomorrow. There are exceptions. In the following pages, however, the authors attempt to point out a few characteristics of behavior that are common enough to make generalizations about.

These may help you to understand American society and get along in it more easily. Later essays will deal with the even more difficult question of beliefs and attitudes. In these essays students should not misinterpret the use of the term America as applied to the people of the United States to mean that these Americans think that they are the only people living in the Western hemisphere. The name United States of America is often shortened to America and thus the people are Americans. The nature of the language also fosters use of the term. One cannot say "United Statesman," as "statesman" has a different meaning, and "United Statesian" would be cumbersome.

Exercise A: Indicate whether each of the following statements is true or false by writing the letter T or F in the space provided.

— 1. "When in Rome, do as the Romans do." is a Roman proverb. and, more important, what their attitudes and beliefs are.

— 2. They have a wide variety of national backgrounds, so there are not bound to be regional and temperamental differences.

— 3. It is easy to make generalizations about American manners and customs.

— 4. In later essays students should misinterpret the use of the term American.

— 5. The name United States of American is often shortened to America.

Exercise B: Give a brief account of the customs of shaking hands in your country.

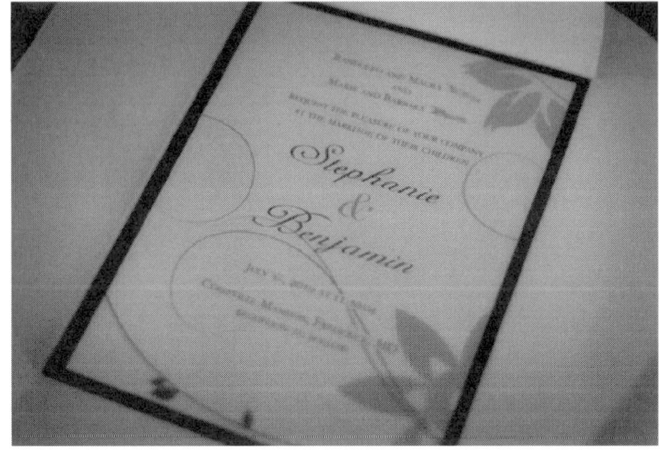
Stephanie
&
Benjamin

INVITATION

1. Useful Words and Idioms

invitation
confusing
unfamiliar with
vague
inhabitant
rural / urban area
relative
champagne
to toast
hospitality
countryside

It is time to leave
It is a pleasure to
Don't mention it
to drop in
to make visits
each other
to be anxious about
to wait for
to be patient with
to have a good time

2. Common Expressions

some common invitations:

Do come over and see us sometime.
Come over anytime. We're always home.
You'll have to stop over and see us sometime.
How about going to the show with me sometime?
Would you care to join me for lunch?

some common remarks when accepting the invitation:

Thanks so much. I'd love to.
That sounds like fun. I'll be over.
I'd love to. What time does it start?
I wouldn't want to inconvenience you.

DIALOGUE

Read the Text:

1. A: Thanks for inviting me to your birthday party.
   B: Thank you for coming.
   A: Here's a small gift for you.
   B: Thanks ever so much. May I open it now?
   A: Of course.
   B: What a cute doll! Oh, thank you.

2. A: Say, what are you doing tomorrow evening?
   B: Why, I don't know. I hadn't thought much about it. Why?
   A: How'd you like to come over to our house for supper?
   B: What time would you like for me to come?
   A: Oh, around 6:30. Is that too late for you?
   B: No, that's fine.
   A: Great! We'll be looking for you then.
   B: Thanks so much for the invitation.
   A: Oh, don't mention it. We're happy to have you over.

Excercise A: Restate your part of the conversation from the text.

1. Thanks for inviting me to your birthday party.
2. Say, what are you doing tomorrow evening?
3. How'd you like to come over to our house for supper?
4. Is that too late for you?
5. Thanks so much for the invitation.

Excercise B: Fill in the blanks.

1. Would you (   ) to join me for lunch?
2. I'll look (   ) to seeing you tomorrow.
3. What time will you be (   ) me?
4. I wouldn't want to put you to any (   ).
5. That's (   ) with me. I'll meet you then.

COMPOSITION

Read the Text:

There is one aspect of the American system of invitations that is sometimes confusing to visitors unfamiliar with the culture. Americans are very likely to make a vague statement like, "Come back and see us soon," or "Drop in any time." Such invitations are genuine and sincere, and coming from an inhabitant of a small town or rural area, may usually be accepted literally. But the visiting habits of many other families, especially those living in urban areas, are somewhat different: It is not customary for most Americans to make unannounced visits to anyone's home, except those of close relatives and very intimate friends. An invitation to "come back again" is almost always sincere, but before actually making such a return visit, the guest should write or telephone the family to make sure that his visit will be convenient.

Exercise A: Answer the questions 1 to 5 tn complete sentences.

1. What aspect of the American system of invitations is there?
2. What are American very likely to make?
3. Aren't the visiting habits of many other families somewhat different?
4. Isn't it customary for the American to make unannounced visits to anyone's home?
5. Why should guest write or telephone the family?

Exercise B: Make sentences following the example.

Ex: there / aspect / invitations
There is one aspect of the American system of invitations.

1. invitations / come / inhabitant
2. living / areas / different
3. customary / Americans / unannounced
4. invitation / is / sincere
5. guest / write / family

READING

Read the Text:

It is a pleasure to write this letter because it gives me an opportunity to tell you how much I enjoyed your hospitality last weekend. This was my first visit to an American family. At first, I was anxious about my limited English and my knowledge of the customs. Then, I saw you and your children waiting for me at the station with warm smiles of welcome on your faces. I immediately knew that everything was going to be all right. You and your wonderful family put me at ease right away.

There are many happy memories of the weekend that I will keep with me forever. How can I mention them all? Above all, I will remember that you made me feel "right at home." There were so many new and different things for me to see and do. I particularly enjoyed driving through the countryside with Mr. Johnson and you and seeing the changing colors of the leaves on the trees. I liked playing baseball and Monopoly with your son, Jimmy and Joey.

They were very patient with me and full of fun. Tell them I will teach them how to play soccer next time. I also had a good time at the Community Square Dance on Saturday night. It was my first square dance, and I cannot forget how friendly and kind everyone was.

Exercise A: Indicate whether each of the following statements is true or false by writing the letter T or F in the space provided.

— 1. This was my first visit to your family.
— 2. I immediately knew that nothing was going to be all right.
— 3. There are many happy memories of the weekend that I will keep with me forever.
— 4. I liked playing baseball and Monopoly with your sons, Jimmy and Joey.
— 5. I also had a good time at the Community Square Dance on Sunday night.

Exercise B: If you have to refuse an invitation, you should do it gracefully. What is your graceful expression?

HOLIDAY

1. Useful Words and Idioms

to spend
to decorate
to celebrate
customary
to invite
to share
holiday / vacation
traditional
present / gift
to fly to
to be sorry for
to go sightseeing
used to
to share the meal
to join
to wake up
out of season

2. Common Expressions

American Holidays:

New Year's Day (January 1)
Lincoln's Birthday (February 12)
Saint Valentine's Day (February 14)
Washington's Birthday (February 22)
Easter Sunday
Memorial Day (May 30)
Independence Day (July 4)
Labor Day (the first Monday in September)
Armistice Day (November 11)
Thanksgiving Day (the fourth Thursday in November)
Christmas Day (December 25)

DIALOGUE

Read the Text:

1. A: How did you spend your vacation?
   B: I did so many things that I'm still tired.
   A: That's how it is with vacations. A person doesn't really rest.
   B: I travelled too much, and tried to see many things.
   A: Are you sorry for that?
   B: No, I'm not.

2. A: I'm flying to Denver.
   B: Isn't that a long trip for a weekend?
   A: Oh, we have a long weekend this week. Friday is a holiday. I don't have to go to school.
   B: Maybe I can go to town on Friday. I want to buy some things.
   A: You can't buy much on a holiday.
   B: Does anyone work on holidays?
   A: A few doctors and dentists wort on holidays.
   B: Are there many holidays?
   A: We have many holidays; New Year's Day, Lincoln's Birthday, Saint Valentine's Day, Washington's Birthday, Easter Sunday, Memorial Day, Independence Day, Labor Day, Columbus Day, Halloween, Thanksgiving Day, and Christmas Day.

Exercise A: Restate your part of the conversation from the text.

1. How did you spend your vacation?
2. Are you sorry for that?
3. Isn't that a long trip for a weekend?
4. Does anyone work on holidays?
5. Are there many holidays?

Exercise B: Fill in the blanks.

1. Lincoln's Birthday is usually just remembered—not (   ).

2. Easter Sunday is a moveable (   ) holiday which celebrates Christ's Resurrection.
3. Labor Day come on the first Monday in (   ).
4. Armistice Day is the anniversary of the signing of the (   ) of World War 1 in 1918.
5. Now Halloween is a (   ) holiday.

COMPOSITION

Read the Text:

Thanksgiving Day is always celebrated on the fourth Thursday of November. It is the most traditional of American holidays.

The first Thanksgiving was held in Massachusetts in 1621. After a year of great hardship, the Pilgrim colonists wanted to give thanks and invited some Indians to join them in a big feast. Today the holiday is still celebrated as a day for giving thanks. It is a day of family reunion and it is customary to invite friends to share the meal.

In some large cities, there are carnival parades for children. In other cities, there are important football games that are played on Thanksgiving Day.

Exercise A: Answer the questions 1 to 5 in complete sentences.

1. When was the first Thanksgiving held?
   Where was it held?
2. Why did the Pilgrims want to give to God?
3. Whom did they invite to join them tn a big feast?
4. How is the holiday still celebrated today?
5. What are there in some large cities?

Exercise B: Make sentences following the example.

Ex: invited / Indian / join / feast
They invited their Indian friends to join them in a big feast.

1. Thanksgiving / celebrate / fourth
2. most / traditional / holidays
3. day / family / reunion
4. customary / invite / meal
5. other cities / football / Thanksgiving

READING

Read the Text:

Last summer I spent a two-week vacation in Miami Beach, Florida. My roommate and I flew to Miami from New York in three hours. It was the first time for both of us, and we went there because the rates are lower out-of-season. We stayed at an air-conditioned luxury hotel tn the beach. We slept late every morning and then had breakfast outdoors near the pool. When the weather was not too hot, we used to go sightseeing in the morning. We visited the Seaquarium, the campus of the University of Miami, and the Everglades. In the afternoons; we used to go swimming in the ocean or the pool, lie in the sun, or go water-skiing. After dinner in the evening, we used to go dancing in a discothque or watch the entertainment in the night clubs. The weather was very good every day, and the two weeks went by too quickly. We were both very sorry when the vacation ended.

Exercise A: Indicate whether each of the following statement is true or false by writing the letter T or F in the space provided.

— 1. My roommate and I flew to New York from Miami in the three hours.
— 2. We stayed at an inexpensive hotel on the beach.
— 3. When the weather was too hot, we used to go sightseeing in the morning.
— 4. After dinner tn the evening we used to go dancing in a discothque or watch the entertainment tn the night clubs.
— 5. The weather was very good every day, and the two weeks went by too quickly.

Exercise B: What is the most traditional holiday in your country?

BUCURESTI

Lesson 7

TIME

1. Useful Words and Idioms

to get up at
alarm clock
to comb
scrambled eggs
punctuality
public affairs
nuisance
clock / calendar time
arbitrary subdivision
hour / minute / second

to be ready to
to take a shower
to get dressed
to work in
on time
to be given to
to set out
to be based on
to be associated with
to keep an eye on

2. Common Expressions

7 minutes slow / fast
every 7 minutes
before 7
by 7
5 to 7
5 past 7
7 o'clock sharp
2:45 : Two-forty five.
A quarter till three
A quarter of three.
A quarter to three.
Fifteen minutes till three.
Fifteen minutes of three.
Fifteen minutes to three.

6:10 six-ten
Ten minutes past six
Ten minutes after six
What time is it?
What's the time?
What time do you have?
Can you tell me the time?

DIALOGUE

Read the Text:

1. A: What time does your meeting begin?
   B: It begins at eight o'clock. What time is it now?
   A: Six twenty-five.
   B: I have to go now. I don't want to be late.
   A: You won't be late. It's early.
   B: O. K.

2. A: What time is it?
   B: My watch says six ten.
   A: I have to buy a new watch.
   B: What's wrong with your watch?
   A: It doesn't keep good time. It gains five minutes a day.
   B: You'd better have it fixed.
   A: How long will it take?
   B: About two days.
   A: Could you also change the crystal?
   B: Very well, sir.

Exercise A: Restate your part of the conversation from the text.

1. What time does your meeting begin?
2. It begins at eight o'clock. What time is it now?
3. What's wrong with your watch?
4. How long will it take?
5. Could you also change the crystal?

Exercise B: Fill in the blanks.

1. Excuse me, sir. What (   ) do you have?
2. It's a quarter (   ) six.
3. The Korean War broke out (   ) June 25, 1950.
4. They are (   ) their late fifties.
5. I am leaving here the day (   ) tomorrow.

COMPOSITION

Read the Text:

Punctuality is a necessary habit in all public affairs of a civilized society. Without it, nothing could ever be brought to a conclusion; everything would be tn a state of chaos. Only in a sparsely-populated rural community is it possible to disregard it. In ordinary living there can be some tolerance of unpunctuality. The intellectual, who is working on some abstruse problem, has everything coordinated and organized for the matter in hand.

He is therefore forgiven, if late for dinner party. but people are often reproached for unpunctuality when their only fault is cutting things fine. It is hard for energetic, quick-minded people to waste time, so, they are often tempted to finish a job before setting out to keep an appointment. If no accidents occur on the way, like punctured tyres, diversions of traffic, sudden descent of frog, they will be on time.

They are often more industrious, useful citizens than those who are never late. The over-punctual can be as much a trial to others are the the unpunctual. The guest who arrives half an hour too soon is the greatest nuisance. Some friends of my family had this irritating habit. The only thing to do was ask them to come half an hour later than the other guests. Then they arrived just then we wanted them.

Exercise A: Answer the questions 1 to 5 in complete sentence.

1. Why is punctuality a necessary habit in all public affairs?
2. Is it hard for energetic people to waste time?
3. In what cases of accident won't they be on time?
4. Is the guest who arrives half an hour early the greatest nuisance?
5. Do you think being early means wasting a little time?

Exercise B: Make sentences following the example.

Ex: punctuality / necessary / affairs
Punctuality is a necessary habit in all public affairs.

1. sparsely–populated / community / disregard
2. forgiving / if / dinner
3. they / tempted / appointment
4. they / industrious / than
5. some / family / irritating

READING

Read the Text:

In the measurement of time there are two fundamental units: the day, which is based on the rotation of the earth, and the year, which is the period of the earth's revolution around the sun. The day is the basis of clock time; the year, the basis of calendar time.

The month and the week are associated with the motion of the moon around the earth, but they are not measured by observation of the moon. A week is a period of seven days, and a month is a period varying between 28 and 31 days. Hours, minutes, and seconds are just arbitrary subdivisions of a day: an hour is one twenty-fourth of a day, a minute is one sixtieth of an hour, and a second is one sixtieth of a minute. Any other members might have been used as divisors, and any other names might have been given to these fractions of a day; but these particular combinations work out quite well and are widely used throughout the would. The precise measurement of time is a part of modern living. Plane and train schedules, athletic events, and radio and television programs are carefully timed. School days and workdays are limited by the clock, and in many cases pay rates are in terms of dollars per hour. The scientist in his laboratory and the navigator at sea need exact measurements of time in making their calculations; homemakers, in cooking and baking, keep an eye on the clock. scientists use divisions of time ranging from a microsecond (1/1,000,000 of a second) to millions of years.

Exercise A: Indicate weather each of the following statements is true or false by writing the letter T or F in the space provided

— 1. The day is the basis of clock time.
— 2. A month is a period of 30 days.
— 3. An hour is one twenty-fourth of a month.
— 4. Plane and train schedules are carefully timed.
— 5. Scientists use divisions of time ranging from a microsecond to millions of years.

Exercise B: What is the difference in meaning between solar and lunar?

Lesson 8

PARTY

1. Useful Words and Idioms

to invite
birthday
to celebrate
guest
to overstay
homecoming
gossip
to bless
gift / present
welcome
to fall on
to be kept secret
to represent
to blow out
to sit down to dinner
to sit around and talk
to be favored by
to follow the lead of
enjoyable

2. Common Expressions

some common compliments while eating:

This is a delicious meal.
My, the fish is delicious.

some common remarks after eating:

The dinner was wonderful.
I enjoyed the dinner so much.
That's the best meal I've had in a long time.
Thank you much for the delicious dinner.

DIALOGUE

Read the Text:

1. A: Are you free Thursday afternoon?
   B: Oh, yes. Why?
   A: I'm giving a birthday party. Can you come?
   B: Thank you. I'd love to come. What time?
   A: About two-thirty.
   B: I'm afraid I can't make it that early.
   Would three-thirty be okay?
   A: That's perfectly all right.
2. A: Hi, Emma! Are you doing anything tonight?
   B: Nothing special.
   A: How about going to a party with me?
   B: That's a great idea. Who else is going?
   A: John and Susan.
   B: Oh, good. I like both of them. What time are we going?
   A: well, around eight. How's that?
   B: Fine. See you at eight then.
   A: See you later.

Exercise A: Restate your part of the conversation from the text.

1. Are you free Thursday afternoon?
2. I'm giving a birthday party. Can you come?
3. Would three-thirty be all right?
4. Are you doing anything tonight?
5. How about going to a party with me?

Exercise B: Fill in the blanks.

1. Let me pay this time. Oh, it's my (　　) today.
2. My birthday falls (　　) February 23.
3. Monday's child is (　　) in the face.
4. Thursday's child has far to (　　).
5. (　　) on your birthday!

COMPOSITION

Read the Text:

All my aunts, uncles, cousins, nephews, and nieces gather for a family homecoming. We always invite some friends to join us. Everyone is glad to see everyone else and there is a very busy exchange of gossip. The women soon disappear into the kitchen to help my grandmother prepare the dinner. The men, meanwhile, settle down to watch a football game on television or to discuss business or politics. If the weather permits, some of the more athletic men go outside to play ball with the children. At about four o'clock we all sit down to diner. My grandfather gives thanks for the blessings we have received and then he starts to carve the turkey. We always have the traditional dinner of stuffed turkey, cranberry sauce, apple cider, sweet potatoes, chestnuts, and pumpkin pie. After dinner, no one can move and we all sit around and talk, play word games, or tell jokes until it is time to go home.

Exercise A: Answer the questions 1 to 5 tn complete sentences.

1. Whom do you always invite?
2. Where do the women soon disappear to?
3. Why do they disappear into the kitchen?
4. It the weather permits, what do the more athletic men do?
5. What happens after dinner?

Exercise B: Make sentences following the example.

Ex: every / glad / else
Everyone is to see everyone else.

1. we / invite / join
2. settle down / watch / television
3. four o'clock / watch / television
4. grandfather / thanks / blessings
5. we / around / talk

READING

Read the Text:

As guests continue to arrive, it has been considered polite for the men tn the group to stand when a women enters the room and continue to stand until she is seated. This is still observed in many homes. However, some young people and some groups of older folk that make a point of stressing equality of the sexes no longer observe the custom. A visitor will be sensitive to each situation and follow the lead of the Americans present.

Following dinner, guests usually stay for two or three hours, but the thoughtful person is careful not to overstay his or her welcome. The host and hostess may urge a guest to stay longer in order to be polite, but most dinner parties break up at about 11 o'clock.

As the guest leave, it is the custom to thank the hostess for a very pleasant evening. One may say anything that truly expresses appreciation. Common expressions are, "Good-bye. It was so nice of you to have me," or "Good-bye. It's been a thoroughly enjoyable evening," or "Thank you. I've had such a good time." For larger favors than a dinner party, such as an overnight or weekend visit, it is customary to send a thank-you note (which is called a "bread-and-butter letter"), and quite often people later send a small gift such as a box of candy or some flowers as a sign of their appreciation.

Exercise A: Indicate whether each of the following statements is true or false by writing the letter T or F in the space provided.

1. As guests continue to leave, it has been considered polite for the women in the group to stand.
2. A visitor will be sensitive to each situation and follow the lead of the Americans present.
3. The host may urge a guest to stay shorter to be polite.
4. One may say anything that truly expresses appreciation.
5. As the guests leave, Common expressions are "Good evening."

Exercise B: If you could spend your birthday as your wished, would you have a birthday party?

THEATER

1. Useful Words and Idioms

theater
movie / motion-picture
to dream of
ticket
lobby
actor / actress
tragedy
make-up
to flock
except for
to go and see
by the way
That's enough for me.
to be used to
What's on?
to gain in popularity
to be viewed
to take one's place
to meet the competition

2. Common Expressions

first-run film
audience
plot
documentary
double feature
animated cartoon
stage
cast
preview / private
extra
performance
movie / film
musical
scene
theme song
lobby
intermission
comedy

DIALOGUE

Read the Text:

1. A: Let's go to a movie.
   B: What's playing?
   A: There's an American picture at the Scala, and a Korean picture at the Kukdo.
   B: What's the American picture about?
   A: It's about life in America.
   B: That's enough for me. Let's go and see it.

2. A: By the way, what are you going to do this afternoon?
   B: Oh, I'm not sure.
   A: Well, I have three tickets for a musical play at the Kukje. Would you like to come along? You may bring a friend, too.
   B: That'd be very nice. Thanks a lot. What time shall we meet you?
   A: The play starts at one-thirty, so let's meet in front of the Kukje at one-fifteen.
   B: All right. We'll try to be there by one-fifteen.
   A: That's all right. You're usually late. I'm used to it.

Exercise A: Restate your part of the conversation from the text.

1. Let's go to a movie.
2. There's an American picture at the Scala, and a Korean picture at the Kukdo.
3. By the way, what are you going to do this afternoon?
4. I have three tickets for a musical play. Would you like to come along?
5. Let's meet in front of the Kukje at one-fifteen.

Exercise B: Fill in the blanks.

1. O. K. What's (   )?
2. Movie do far more than (   ).
3. Motion pictures play an important part in our lives.
4. Movies are really a long series of (   ) pictures.
5. (   ) films are wonderful for reporting history.

COMPOSITION

Read the Text:

Even in the early English theater the acting companies had certain players who took the important roles and became known as stars. The public flocked to see a star in each of his roles, and the art of the actor seemed much greater than the art of the playwright who created the character played. The star system has continued into the present. During the nineteenth century people went to the theater to see the popular stars — not to see and hear the plays in which they appeared. The famous actors toured Europe and America with their own companies or appeared as guest stars with local companies.

The style of acting was usually declamatory. The actors addressed the audience in their long speeches, using highly dramatic gestures. The modern style of controlled, realistic acting, in which the actor never steps out of his role and usually underplays emotional scenes, is gaining in popularity, but some actors and actresses still prefer the more heroic style.

Exercise A: Answer the questions 1 to 5 in complete sentences.

1. What had certain players even in the early English theater?
2. Why did the public flock?
3. Did the art of the playwright seem much greater than the art of the actor?
4. Why did people go to the theater during the nineteenth century?
5. How did the actors address the audience?

Exercise B: Make sentences following the example.

Ex: players / took / important / known
Certain players took the important roles and became known as stars.

1. star / continued / present
2. famous / toured / companies
3. style / acting / declamatory
4. actor / steps / underplays
5. actors and actresses / prefer / heroic

READING

Read the Text:

Perhaps no single change has had greater impact on the motion-picture industry than the rapid growth of television. In oder to meet the competition, many studios began to produce wide-screen movies and three-dimensional movies (which could be viewed only through special spectacles distributed to the theater audiences). Cinerama featured a curved wide screen on which the movie was shown from three different projectors, plus a much-improved stereophonic sound system. The purpose of this combination was to make the viewer feel that he was in the midst of the scene by using his side vision and by hearing sounds from all directions. Cinemascope, another wide-screen system, achieved similar results by using widespread the projection over a wider screen. Despite these innovations, television seriously cut theater attendance. The total number of movie theaters in the United States dropped from 19,000 to about 16,000. About 5,000 of these were outdoor drive-in theaters.

The United States films, however, have remained popular in Canada (which has over 2,000 theaters) and in other countries. Several countries have become noted for production of outstanding feature films. Italy has created some remarkably interesting films, as have Great Britain, France, Sweden, Russia, India, and Japan.

Exercise A: Indicate whether each of the following statements is true or false by writing the letter T or F in the space provided.

1. Perhaps the rapid growth of motion picture has had the greatest impact on the television industry.
2. Cinerama didn't feature a curved wide screen.
3. Cinerama achieved similar results by using wide angle lenses to film the production.
4. Despite these innovations, television seriously cut theater attendance.
5. Several countries have become noted for production of outstanding feature films.

Exercise B: Which do you like better, an American picture or a Korea picture?

Lesson 10

SPORTS

1. Useful Words and Idioms

favorite
fan
intercollegiate game
to reach
to win / lose
recreation
opposing team
spectator
participant
to throw
major/minor
millions of
to be called off
to be put off
to be going to
as well as
to talk about
to try for
to look up to
to make a high score
to be played by
to be shaped like

2. Common Expressions

volleyball
tennis
hockey
boxing
basketball
swimming
ping-pong
football / soccer
climbing
fishing
skating
baseball
to take part in / participate in
go in for a sport
to broadcast a sports events
sports(sport) car
sports magazine
sports commentator
sports equipment / sporting goods

DIALOGUE

Read the Text:

1. A: How was the intercollegiate ball last week?
   B: It was called off on account of rain.
   A: That's too bad. Then when did they decide to hold it?
   B: They finally held it last Saturday.
   A: How was the game?
   B: Our team won.
   A: Congratulations!
2. A: They're exchanging strong baseline shots.
   B: Borg is playing in the back court.
   His serve is a cannon ball.
   A: Connors breaks the opponent's service and strong counterattacks.
   A: Borg volleyed spectacularly.
   B: Connors resorts fast and gives a beauty.
   A: They reach a 5-5 tie.

Exercise A: Restate your part of the conversation from the text.

1. How was the intercollegiate ball game last week?
2. That's too bad. Then when did they decide to hold it?
3. How was the game?
4. Who broke the opponent's service?
5. How did Borg volley?

Exercise B: Fill in the blanks.

1. The baseball game was put ( ) till the next day.
2. Sports include all athletics as well as almost all other games, contests, and ( ).
3. Millions of Americans fish for ( ).
4. A sport in which large numbers of people watch a few persons play is called a ( ) sport.
5. The rise of skiing as a major ( ) sport can be traced to the ten years following Would War 11.

COMPOSITION

Read the Text:

American football is played by two teams of eleven men each. It is played on a rectangular field with a line across it every ten yards. (Because of this, the field is often called a gridiron.) At each end of the field there is an end zone, with a goal post which is shaped like the letter "H". The ball is oval-shaped.

It is often called a pigskin because it is covered in leather. The object of the game is to get the ball across the goal line of the opposing team. When a team has the ball, it has four chances called downs, to advance the ball ten yards. This may be done by running with the ball, throwing it, or both. If the team cannot advance ten yards in four tries, the other team gets the ball. If a player on one team drops the ball and it is gotten by a member of the other team, then the latter team gets to keep it and try for an advance of ten yards.

Exercise A: Answer the questions 1 to 5 in complete sentences.

1. How many players does a football team have?
2. What does a football field look like?
3. What does the ball look like?
4. What is the object of the game?
5. In football, what is a down?

Exercise B: Make sentences following the example.

Ex: American / played / teams
American football is played by two teams of eleven men each.

1. end / there / zone
2. may / done / running
3. if / team / advance / tries
4. player / drops / gotten
5. keep / advanced / yards

READING

Read the Text:

The fall season also sees the World Series in baseball to determine the champion professional team of the nation. Baseball professionals are organized into major and minor leagues. The best players from the minor leagues are recruited into a ball club (team)that is a member of either the National League or the American League. The team that wins the most games in its league then, in October, plays the champion of the other league in the World Series, a series of games to determine the best team in the nation. Heroes in baseball are talked about and remembered as in perhaps no other sport. School children look up to the pitcher or batter who is currently making a high score for his team.

Although no other game is exactly like baseball, perhaps the one most nearly like it is the English game of cricket. In baseball there are nine players on each side. The two teams alternate at bat (the offense) and in the field (the defense). Each pair of turns at bat is called an inning. There are nine innings in each game.

Not only is baseball played by professional teams but by children tn their neighborhoods and by high school and college teams in the spring. It is also played by adults as amateurs.

Exercise A: Indicate whether each of the following statements is true or false by writing the letter T or F in the space provided.

—1. Baseball professionals are organized into Atlantic and Pacific leagues.
—2. Every team can play the champion of the World Series.
—3. School children look down to the pitcher currently making a high score for his team.
—4. In baseball there are eighteen players on each side.
—5. Baseball is played only by professional teams.

Exercise B: Give a brief account of your favorite winter sports.

Lesson 11

TELEPHONE

1. Useful Words and Idioms

to call up / ring up	to pick up
operator	the wrong number
to dial	would like to
volume	neither A nor B
conversation	to lift off
to lift	to hang up
to make appointments	whether A or B
information	to look up
business	in front of
message	
receive	

2. Common Expressions

extension telephone	to telephone / phone / make a phone call to
interphone	
person to person call	to get/receive a (tele) phone call from
station to station call	to dial the wrong number / the numbers
long distance call	to get / call sb. on the phone (line)
collect call	to be busy
receiver	to be off the line
phone booth	
zip code	
telephonograph	

DIALOGUE

Read the Text:

1. A: May I speak to Robert MacDonald, please?
   B: I'm sorry. You must have the wrong number.
   A: There's no one here by that name.
   B: Is this Sterling 3-4715?
   A: No, this is Sterling 3-4714.
   B: Oh, I'm sorry.
   A: That's all right.
2. A: Operator! I want to make a long-distance cal to Seoul.
   B: All right. Your number in Seoul, please.
   A: The number is 359-6317.
   B: Whom do you want to speak to, sir?
   A: Please make it a station to station call.
   B: Then you dial yourself.

Exercise A: Restate your part of the conversation from the text.

1. May I speak to Robert MacDonald, please?
2. Is this Sterling 3-4715.
3. Operator! I want to make a long-distance call.
4. All right. Your number in Seoul lease.
5. Please make it a station to station call.

Exercise B: Fill in the blanks.

1. Hello. may I speak to Mr. Wilson, please?
   Yes, I'll (　) him.
2. Give me a (　) when you get time.
3. I must (　) my wife to tell her I won't be home for dinner tonight.
4. I'd like to (　) Denver, Colorado 4-7963.
5. The person to person call means that you will talk only to the one person you are (　).

COMPOSITION

Read the Text:

The telephone is important to Americans both for business and for personal reasons. With the telephone you can get in touch with people quickly, whether they are in the city or across the continent. The business world of today could hardly live without the telephone. Personal telephone calls are very important, too. You can often call up a friend or relative and have a pleasant talk, when you can not visit in person.

In most parts of the United States there are dial phones. This means that you look up the number you want to call and then dial it. In parts of the country where they don't have dial phones yet, you look up the number you want to call, pick up the phone, and when the operator answers, tell her the number you want.

Exercise A: Answer the questions 1 to 5 in complete sentences.

1. Why is the telephone important to Americans?
2. What world could hardly live without the telephone?
3. What can you do when you cannot visit in person?
4. In most parts of the United States are there dial phones?
5. What do you do where they don't have dial phones yet?

Exercise B: Make sentences following the example.

Ex : They / across / continent
They are in the city or across the continent.

1. telephone / touch / quickly
2. personal / calls / important
3. you / friend / when
4. most parts / there / dial phones
5. operator / tell / the number

READING

Read the Text:

In America practically every factory, company, school, and private home has a telephone. This makes it very easy to call anyone and ask for information, make appointments, or you can even order groceries by phone if you want.

Almost all private telephones are dial phones. This means there is a dial on the front of the phone where you dial each number of the phone number of the person you want to call.

You lift the receiver off the hook first, then dial the number and wait to hear it ring. If the line is busy, you will not hear it ring, but will hear a buzzing sound instead. This means you will have to hang up and wait a while before you try again.

In towns of average size the telephone numbers are usually four or five numbers long, but in large towns the numbers often have a word before the numbers. For example, the number might be Lincoln 46371 instead of just 46371. This means that you take the first two letters of the word (in this case "LI") and dial them first. Then dial the number after that. In most cases the number will be written Lincoln 46371 or maybe even just LI46371.

If you have trouble and cannot dial the person you want, dial "O" for the operator, and when she answers explain your problem to her and she will help you.

Exercise A: Indicate whether each of the following statements is true or false by writing the letter T or F in the space provided.

1. In America practically every factory, company, school, and private home has a telephone.
2. Almost all private telephones are dial phones.
3. You dial the number, then lift the receiver off the hook.
4. In large towns the numbers often have a word before the numbers
5. If you have trouble and cannot dial the person you want, dial "O" for the educator.

Exercise B: What is the meaning of "person to person" call?

Lesson 12

SHOPPING

1. Useful Words and Idioms

sports jacket
to wear
to measure
parking lot
customer
errand
beauty shop
saleslady
supermarket

to loot for
to be window shopping
with enthusiasm
to walk out of the shop
That's too much.
Here's the money.
to go shopping
on the fifth floor
to go downtown

2. Common Expressions

What size shoes do you wear?
socks
stockings
suit
dress
hat
belt
shirt

I'd like to try on this sweater.
pair of pants
overcoat
raincoat

Is this toothpaste on sale today?
shaving cream
soap
hair oil
article
merchandise

That suit looks very good.
on you.
too big
too small
just right

DIALOGUE

Read the Text:

1. A: May I help you, please?
   B: Yes, I'm looking for a jacket.
   A: What kind of jacket did you have in mind?
   B: A sports jacket.
   A: We have a very good selection of sports jackets. What size do you wear?
   B: I am not sure of my size. Perhaps you'd better measure me.
   A: All right. You wear a size 34.

2. A: I'd like two pairs of these socks, size twelve.
   B: What color?
   A: Black, I guess. I also want to buy a shirt, size 15.
   A: A dress shirt, please.
   B: That comes to eight-fifty, including tax.
   A: Can you change a twenty?
   B: Sure. Here's your change.

Exercise A: Restate your part of the conversation from the text.

1. May I help you, please?
2. What kind of jacket did you have in mind?
3. What size do you wear?
4. Would you like a dress shirt or a sport shirt?
5. Can you change a twenty?

Exercise B: Fill in the blanks.

1. No, thanks, I'm ( ) looking.
2 How ( ) is this?
3. This one will ( ).
4. No, that's not quite what I'm ( ) for.
5. No, this ( ) in any other colors?

COMPOSITION

Read the Text:

A shopping center is a group of stores with a big parking lot, located in the suburbs. Shopping centers have grown up fairly recently since co many people have moved out of the city to the suburbs. It is more convenient for people to shop near their homes than it is for them to go downtown. It is also convenient for people to be able to park once and do all their errands and shopping.

Of course, not all shopping centers have exactly the same stores, but a typical shopping center in the suburbs of a large city would probably have a supermarket (that is, a large grocery store), a branch of a downtown department store, a ten-cent store, a drug-store, a barber shop, a beauty shop, a dry cleaner's, and perhaps also a hardware store, a bank, a flower store and a book store.

Exercise A: Answer the questions 1 to 5 in complete sentence.

1. What is a shopping center?
2. Why have shopping centers grown up recently in the suburbs?
3. Do all shopping centers have exactly the same stores?
4. What kinds of stores does a typical shopping center have?
5. Describe each store.

Exercise B: Make sentences following the example.

Ex: shopping / grown / fairly
Shopping centers have grown up fairly recently.

1. shopping center / group / parking
2. many people / move / suburbs
3. convenient / people / shop
4. It / convenient / park
5. typical / have / supermarket

READING

Read the Text:

One day last week, Mrs. Clark went shopping. On her way home she saw a dress in a window of a small shop. Well, she fell in love with it. She said, "That dress is perfect for me." So she went into the shop and asked a saleslady, "How much is that cotton dress in the window?" "It's $35.00" answered the saleslady. Mrs. Clark then thought. "$35,00 for a cotten dress! John won't like that." So she decided not to buy the dress that time. She'd wait until later.

When her husband came home that evening, she told him about the beautiful cotton dress in the window. "I saw it in a shop this morning. It's really lovely and . . . ." "And you want to buy it," said Mr. Clark. "How much does it cost?" "$35.00" she answered. "$35.00" she answered. "$35.00 for a cotton dress? No! That's too much!"

Well, Mrs. Clark didn't take "No" for an answer. Every evening after that, Mrs. Clark spoke of nothing else, but the dress. That's all Mr. Clark heard from his wife so at last, after a week he said, "Oh, buy the dress! Here's the money!" But the next evening when Mr. Clark came home he asked, "Well where is it?" "Where's what?" asked Mrs. Clark. "You know what — the famous dress. Did you buy it?" "No!" "Why not?" he asked. "Well, it was still in the window of the shop after a week so I thought, Nobody else wants it, so I don't either."

Exercise A: Indicate whether each of the following statements is true or false by writing the letter T or F in the space provided.

—1. On her way home Mrs. Clark saw a dress in a window of a small shop.
—2. Mrs. Clark didn't decide to buy the cotton dress.
—3. John thought the dress is too cheap.
—4. Well, Mrs. Clark took "No" for an answer.
—5. After all, Mrs. Clark bought the cotton dress.

Exercise B: What is the principal attraction of the supermarket to the average customer?

Lesson 13

FLOWER

1. Useful Words and Idioms

hot / green house	How long does it take?
to handle	to be related to
moisture	such as
assortment	to be attractive to
common / scientific name	to look down into
scent	to contain
garlic / shallot / chive	to be recognized as
arrangement	to be necessary for
scent / perfume / sachet	
bud / seed / petal / ovary	

2. Common Expressions

Flowers for the Months:

month	exoteric	esoteric
January	wild rose	snowdrop
February	pink	primrose
March	violet	
April	easter lily	
May	Lily of the valley	Hawthorne
June	rose	morning-glory
July	daisy	hop or nasturtium
August	water lily	
September	poppy	
October	cosmos	
November	chrysanthemum	
December	holly	

DIALOGUE

Read the text:

1. A: Do you only handle out flowers?
   B: We also handle potted plants.
   A: Let me see some of them.
   B: This way to the hot house, ma'am.
   A: How beautiful they are!
   What is the name of these flowers?
   B: Petunia, Ma'am. They are various colored.
   A: How often should I give water?
   B: Once a day in the morning.

2. A: What do you call this orchid?
   B: Catteleya.
   A: It has very strong scent.
   B: And it also keeps flower for a month.
   A: How can I grow it?
   B: It needs suitable moisture and temperature.
   A: Like a fair lady.
   B: It's the Queen of the Flowers.

Exercise A: Restate your part of the conversation from the text.

1. Do you only handle out flowers?
2. Let me show some of them.
3. How often should I give water?
4. What do you call this orchid?
5. How can I grow it?

Exercise B: Fill in the blanks.

1. How much are these flowers (   )?
2. How long will it take when buds (   ) out into flowers?
3. We (   ) a wide assortment.
4. Let me have a (   ) of carnations.
5. Please order one (   ) me.

COMPOSITION

Read the Text:

People who enjoy the beauty of flowers in a garden may also enjoy the pleasure of flower arrangements for the house. Making a flower arrangement is not difficult. It just takes practice, the use of a few rules, simple tools, and some imagination. Besides flowers, the arrangement may include seeds, weeds, dried foliage, and fresh fruits. Figurines, screens, driftwood, or other objects may also be made a part of the arrangement.

First you must decide where your arrangement is to be put when it is completed. The flowers and the container should blend well and add beauty where they are placed. Against a wall, the arrangement should be tall enough to look well. On a dining table it should be low enough that anyone seated at the table can see over the flowers. On a low table the arrangement should be attractive to anyone looking down into it.

Exercise A: Answer the questions 1 to 5 in the complete sentences

1. What kind of people may also enjoy the pleasure of flower arrangements for the house?
2. Making a flower arrangement is easy, isn't it?
3. What must you decide first when your arrangement is completed?
4. How should the arrangement be done on a dining table?
5. How should we arrange flowers on a low table?

Exercise B: Make sentences following the example.

Ex: people / enjoy / pleasure / arrangements / house
People may also enjoy the pleasure of flower arrangements for the house.

1. making / arrangements / difficult
2. objects / made / arrangement
3. flowers / container/blend
4. arrangement / tall / look
5. arrangement / attractive / looking

READING

Read the Text:

The beauty of flowers suggests some of their more obvious uses. Flowers have always been the subject of poetry, paintings, music, and architecture. One can scarcely imagine a world without flowers in the gardens, in the fields and woods, and in striking flower arrangements. Flower growing provides an interesting hobby for many people, and is the basis of the great florist industry.

Since ancient times the scent of some flower petals has been used in perfumes and sachets. A red rose and a white rose were chosen as the symbols for opposing forces during the Wars of the Roses in the fifteenth century. Some flowers are recognized the world over as symbols of certain festive occasions. The lily is widely accepted as a flower for the Easter seaton; the poinsettia, for Christmas; and orange blossoms, for weddings.

From flowering plants we get the greater portion of the food that sustains our life. Flowers are necessary for all of our cereal grains, for these grains are the seeds formed by the ovary of the flower. Seeds of flowers also produce the source of some of our favorite beverages—coffee, tea, cocoa, and chocolate. Besides these, capers used for seasoning are preserved flower buds; cauliflower and broccoli are undeveloped flowers of plants of the cabbage family.

Exercise A: Indicate whether each of the following statements is true or false by writing the letter T or F in the space provided.

—1. Flowers were the subject of poetry, paintings, music.
—2. Flower growing provides an interesting hobby for many people.
—3. A red and white rose was chosen as the symbols for opposing forces in the 15th century.
—4. The poinsettia is widely accepted as a flower for the Easter season.
—5. Form flowering plants we get the greater portion of the food that sustains our life.

Exercise B: Name ten flowering plants.

Lesson 14

HOUSING

1. Useful Words and Idioms

to furnish
apartment
rent
downpayment
to arrange
bargain
to design
style
resident
for sale
to inquire about
to pay for electricity
to be looking for
to be painted
to harmonize with
to be anxious to
to be made of glass
to give pleasure

2. Common Expressions

furniture
janitor
chimney
attic
nameplate
fireplace
brick
real estate
parlor
running water
fence
uptown
garage
lease
window sill
eaves
double room
drain
porch
exclusive area
a house for rent
to show around
to command a fine view

DIALOGUE

Read the Text:

1. A: I'd like to inquire about a furnished apartment.
   B: How many rooms, sir?
   A: One double and two single bed rooms with a bath.
   B: How long do you want it for?
   A: About one year.
   B: When do you want it?
   A: Right now, please.
   B: I'm sure one of those would satisfy you.

2. A: Can I take a look?
   B: Certainly. This way, please.
   A: Looks all right. What's the rent?
   B: $400 a month.
   A: Including utilities?
   B: No, sir.
   A: What is the downpayment?
   B: The first and last month rents plus a cleaning charge of $50. It comes to $850.
   A: All right. I'll take it.
   B: I'm glad you like it.

Exercise A: Restate your part of the conversation from the text.

1. I'd like to inquire about a furnished apartment.
2. How long do you want it for?
3. When do you want it?
4. Can I take a look?
5. What is the downpayment?

Exercise B: Fill in the blanks.

1. What floor is the apartment (　)?
2. Does the toilet (　) well?
3. How much do I pay (　) electricity?
4. We're (　) in our rent.
5. I'd like to have a phone (　), please.

COMPOSITION

Read the Text:

Although these buildings represented a new kind of construction, they were usually designed in one or another of the traditional styles, such as Renaissance, Romanesque, or Gothic. The principle that form follows function led in time to a new, simple style in which the structure of the building was not concealed. Vertical lines were usually emphasized, and setbacks, or terraces were used to create a balance of masses and to break the monotony of boxlike construction. Decoration was simple and sparing.

The twentieth century saw new ideas of architecture in all kinds of building. Engineering improvements and new materials made it possible for the architect to experiment with new styles in houses, industrial buildings, stores, hotels, hospitals, schools, and offices. When walls carry no weight, they can be made of glass, aluminum, or any light material that will serve to keep out the weather. An American architect, Frank Lloyed Wright, was one of the creative leaders who taught that any building must be designed to fit its purpose, to harmonize with its site, and also to give pleasure by its form.

Exercise A: Answer the questions 1 to 5 in complete sentences.

1. How many traditional styles of buildings were they designed in?
2. What were used to create a balance of masses?
3. Did the 20th century see new ideas of architecture in all kinds of building?
4. What made it possible for the architect to experiment with new styles in houses, industrial buildings, and offices?
5. What did Frank Lloyed Wright do?

Exercise B: Make the sentences following the example.

Ex: buildings / represented / construction
These building represented a new kind of construction.

1. designed / traditional / styles
2. simple / structure / concealed
3. decoration / simple / sparing
4. material / serve / weather
5. architect / creative / leaders

READING

Read the Text:

Community conservation attracts residents and home owners who do not wish to cut their ties with the old neighborhood; landlords interested in protecting property valued; businessmen, whose old customers are leaving the area and shopping elsewhere; employers, who find it difficult to hire qualified people because of poor policing or lack of decent housing; churches, losing parishioners to outlying regions and finding transients in their place; schools, PTA, service clubs, and civic leaders, anxious to keep the neighborhood attractive to those families who are active in civic affairs. City governments enter the program because most of their income comes from real estate taxes. Slums require many extra services such as fire and police protection, far beyond the ability of run-down neighborhoods to pay for them. The City of Chicago studied the University of Chicago neighborhood, where one of the nation's first extensive, federally-subsidized community conservation programs had been initiated. It found that money spent by the city as its part of the program would be repaid in eight years through higher taxes collected from the improved properties. Another Chicago study showed that slum clearance cost the city three times what it would have cost to conserve the same neighborhood.

Exercise A: Indicate whether each of the following statements is true or false by writing the letter or F in the space provided.

—1. Landlords are interested in protecting property values.
—2. Employers find it easy to hire qualified people because of poor policing or lack of decent housing.
—3. City governments enter the program because most of their income comes from personal estate taxes.
—4. Slums require many extra services, such as fire and police protection, far beyond the ability of run-down neighborhoods to pay for them.
—5. Another Chicago study showed that slum clearance cost the city three times what it would have cost to conserve the same neighborhood.

Exercise A: Give a brief account of a Korean city government.

Lesson 15

FAMILY

1. Useful Words and Idioms

to remember
anniversary
golden wedding
old / age
celebration
step-sister
niece / nephew
niece-in-law
middle-aged
relative / relation

to live at 235 Apple Street
on Orange Street
to grow up
to eat / have / take lunch
a lot of / many
at times
not at all
to have a good time

2. Common Expressions

single / unmarried
widow / widower
bachelor
adult / grown-up
coming-of-age Day
baby / infant
youth
family / families
husband / wife
father / mother
brother / sister
son / daughter

to be / get married to
to be divorced from
to live / remain single
to live a married life
to make / start a home
to visit / call at one's home
to support one's family
to have a large / small family

DIALOGUE

Read the Text:

1. A: Do you have any brothers and sisters, George?
   B: I have one sister, but I don't have any brothers.
   A: Does your sister live with you?
   B: No, she doesn't. She lives in San Francisco.
   A: Is she married?
   B: Yes, she is.

2. A: I'm tired of cooking meals three times a day.
   I wish this custom was done away with — the custom of a wife preparing meals every day!
   B: And of a husband shaving every morning?
   A: Oh, don't be sarcastic!
   B: Say, how about taking a vacation tonight? Let's go out to dinner for once. Then you won't have to cook.
   A: That's a wonderful idea. What restaurant shall we go to?
   B: What about the Ritz? We'll have the most expensive dinner on the menu. What do you think about that?
   A: Oh, darling, that's wonderful! We'll have to do without eggs and bacon for breakfast a whole month!

Exercise A: Restate your part of the conversation from the text.

1. Do you have any brothers and sisters, George?
2. Does your sister live with you?
3. Is she married?
4. And of a husband shaving every morning?
5. What restaurant shall we go to?

Exercise B: Fill in the blanks.

1. Perhaps you think about the kind of ( ) life you want to have when you grow up and marry.
2. ( ) is the father of one's father or mother..
3. Cousin is a ( ) one's uncle or aunt.
4. ( ) is a son of one's brother or sister.
5. ( ) is the father of one's wife or husband.

COMPOSITION

Read the Text:

My name is John Smith. I live 234 Apple Street. I live with my family. We live in a big house. I have two brothers and one sister.

My father is an engineer. My mother is a nurse. We eat breakfast at home. I study history in school. I eat lunch and dinner at home.

My friend's name is Susan Jones. She lives on Orange Street. She lives with her family. They live in an apartment. She has one brother and no sisters. Her father is a lawyer. Her mother is a teacher. They eat breakfast at home. She studies at school. Susan is a good reader. She reads carefully and well. She eats lunch in school. She does not eat lunch at home.

Exercise A: Answer the questions 1 to 5 in complete sentences.

1. Where does he live?
2. What does he study in school?
3. Who is hit friend?
4. Where does she live?
5. How does she read?

Exercise B: Make sentences following the example.

Ex: we / live / house
We live in a big house.

1. I / brothers / sister
2. lunch / dinner / home
3. she / live / Orange Street
4. she / brother / sister
5. she / not eat / home

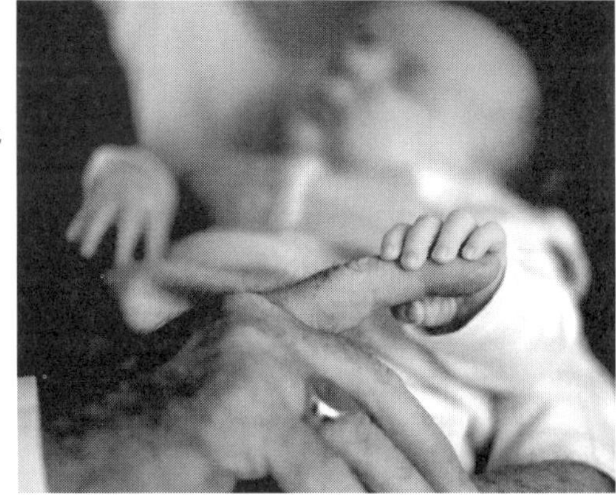

READING

Read the Text:

A golden wedding anniversary is a celebration of fifty years of marriage. Usually there is a big party for all friends and relatives of the married couple. Just think what a lot of people this can be! There are sons and daughters, nieces and nephews, brothers and sisters, cousins, grandchildren—even great-grandchildren. Of course many old friends come, too.

Frequently, members of the family from different towns don't see each other very often. They are glad to come to an anniversary party.

But it can be a time of confusion for the children. It's hard for them to remember the names of all their relatives. "Albert," one mother will say, "This is your cousin George. He's really your second cousin because he's Dorothy's son. Dorothy is my first cousin. Her mother is Aunt Helen, my father's sister."

At times there are stepsisters, half-brothers and nieces-in-law. There are "aunts" and "uncles" who aren't relatives at all, but good friends of the family! It can be very confusing, but everyone has a good time.

Exercise A: Indicate whether each of the following statements is true or false by writing the letter T or F in the space provided.

—1. A golden wedding anniversary is a celebration of thirty years of marriage.
—2. There is a big party for all the friends and relative of the married couple.
—3. Frequently, members of the family from different towns don't see each other very often.
—4. Albert isn't really your second cousin because he's Dorothy's son.
—5. It can be very confusing, but everyone has a good time.

Exercise B: Give a brief account of your family.

Lesson 16

LAUNDRY

1. Useful Words and Idioms

sweater
shirt
to shrink
to starch
linen
garment
to soak
household
refrigerator
to be replaced by
a cake of soap
available for
in coin-operated laundry
to beat on rocks
to prefer not to
to ease
to be unable to

2. Common Expressions and Idioms

iron
wringer
mangle
washing machine
cotton / woolen
sprinkle
sprayer
soapy water
brushing
mending
stain
cloth / material
staple / fiber
darning
cashmere
bleaching powder
starched
soft
rinse

DIALOGUE

Read the Text:

1. A: Did you take your sweater to the laundry last week?
   B: Yes, I did. And it shrank.
   A: Oh, what a shame! What are you going to do now?
   B: I'm going to buy another one.
   A: How much did it cost?
   B: This last one? Let's see ··· $ 20,00.
   A: $20,00! Was it imported?
   B: Yes, it was Italian made.

2. A: Is this the laundromat we're going to use?
   B: Yes, the machines next to the dryer are empty.
   A: There're a few spots on this jacket.
   B: You must not use any bleach or too much soap on the dark clothes.
   A: I soaked them for a few hours in soapy water. But the spots won't come out.
   B: Why don't you have it cleaned?

Exercise A: Restate your part of the conversation from the text.

1. Did you take your sweater to the laundry last week?
2 What are you going to do now?
3. Was it imported?
4. Is this the laundromat we're going to use?
5. But the spots won't come out.

Exercise B: Fill in the blanks.

1. For many years (   ) was the traditional washday.
2. In coin-operated laundries, the individual may wash and (   ) clothes for a small charge for each load.
3. Today, the (   ) remains an important part of our lives.
4. Some automatic machines, called combination washers, (   ) the clothes after they have been washed.
5. Ironing may be done with a dry iron, a (   ) iron, or a mangle which has heated rollers or plates.

COMPOSITION

Read the Text:

For hundreds of years, women washed the family's clothes by soaking them in streams and then beating them on rocks. In some areas this method is still in use. Later, clothes were boiled in outdoor kettles and washed with homemade soaps. Scrubbing the garments up and down on a washboard also became a common laundry method. In the early 1900's, hand-operated washing machines came into existence, but they were replaced by machines powered by water, by gasoline engines, and, finally by those powered by electric motors.

Commercial laundries were common in ancient Greece and Rome about 2,000 years ago. The first commercial laundry in the United States was opened in Oakland, Calif, in 1851 to serve the needs of the miners who came to the area during the gold rush. Coin-operated, industrial, linen-supply, and diaper laundries were largely developed about the middle of the twentieth century.

Exercise A: Answer the questions 1 to 5 in complete sentences.

1. How did women wash the family's clothes for hundreds of years?
2. Is this old-fashioned method still in use?
3. By what were hand-operated washing machines replaced?
4. Where were commercial laundries common about 2,000 years ago?
5. When was the first commercial laundry opened in the U.S.?

Exercise B: Make sentences following the example.

Ex: washed / clothes / soaking
Women washed the family's clothes by soaking them.

1. areas / method / still
2. clothes / boiled / kettles
3. scrubbing / garments / washboard
4. early / hand-operated / existence
5. coin-operated / developed / 20 century

READING

Read the Text:

"Wash on Monday, iron on Tuesday" are the opening words of any old expression describing the occupations of a woman's week.

"Doing the laundry" has always been one of the major household tasks. In most homes the family laundry was done once a week, and in some, where the family was large or there were small children, it was cone more often. For many years Monday was the traditional washday, and women hung the laundered garments and lines to dry on clotheslines strung outdoors or in the basement. The dried clothes which needed to have a smooth finish were then dampened and, later, ironed, usually on Tuesday.

Today, the laundry remains an important part of out lives. Regular laundering keeps soiled garments and lines attractively clean and sweet-smelling, and it helps to prevent the spread of disease. The modern laundry equipment available for use in the home has somewhat eased the housewife"s burden, but doing the laundry is also big business.

Many people prefer not to, or are unable to, do their own laundry. Some have a laundress come to their homes; others have the laundry done in commercial laundries.

Exercise A: Indicate whether each of the following statements is true or false by writing the letter T or F in the space provided.

1. "Wash on Monday, bath on Tuesday" are the opening words of an old expression describing the occupation of a woman's week.
2. In most homes the family laundry was done once a week.
3. The dried clothes which needed to have a smooth finish were then dampened and, later, ironed, usually on Tuesday.
4. The modern laundry equipment available for use in the home has somewhat eased the housewife's burden, but doing the laundry is also big business.
5. Most housewives have the laundry done in commercial laundries.

Exercise B: Briefly explain how you do the family laundry in your home.

Lesson 17

RESTAURANT

1. Useful Words and Idioms

to order
restaurant / cafeteria
waiter / waitress
menu
vegetable
dessert
vanilla

May I take your order?
a glass of milk / water
to be ready for
Would you pass the salt?
help yourself.
on the contrary
to decide on

2. Common Expressions

all-time favorites:
hotdog
hamburger / cheeseburger
fried chicken
barbecued chicken
roast turkey
pork cutlet / chops
baked ham
veal cutlet
sirloin steak
roast beef / prime ribs
meat loaf

It is bitter.
sour
sweet
salty
hot
mellow
tart
fishy
bland
dry
soiled
gamey

DIALOGUE

Read the Text:

1. A: May I take your order, please?
   B: Yes, I think I'd like the roast beef dinner.
   A: You have a choice of two vegetables.
   B: Give me sorn and mashed potatoes.
   A: And what kind of dressing do you want on your salad, sir?
   B: I'll have French dressing, please.
   A: And will you have coffee to drink?
   B: No, I think I'll take a glass of milk.
   A: Thank you.

2. A: Are you ready for your desert, sir?
   B: Yes, what do you have?
   A: We have apple pie, chocolate cake and ice cream.
   B: What kinds of ice cream do you have?
   A: Chocolate, vanilla, strawberry, and orange sherbert.
   B: I'll have vanilla, please.

Exercise A: Restate your part of the conversation from the text.

1. May I take your order, please?
2. You have a choice of two vegetables.
3. And what kind of dressing do you want on your salad, sir?
4. Are you ready for your desert, sir?
5. We have apple pie, chocolate cake and ice cream.

Exercise B: Fill in the blanks.

1. Would you please (   ) the salt?
2. Help (   ).
3. May I get you (   ) of anything?
4. Thank you, I've already eaten too (   ).
5. I (   ) the dinner so much.

COMPOSITION

Read the Text:

In a cafeteria everyone is really his own waiter. You take you own tray and go past the selection of food. There are always many different kinds of food to choose from. You choose just what you want, and every item you choose costs a certain amount. At the end of the line there will be some one to add up your bill and give you a check. You do not pay this check until after you have finished eating and ready to leave. Carry your tray to an empty table and put the plates full of food on the table and sit down and eat your meal.

There is no tipping in a cafeteria. Cafeterias are usually found only in larger towns.

Exercise A: Answer the questions 1 to 5 in complete sentence.

1. Who is really a waiter in a cafeteria?
2. Are there many different kinds of food to choose from?
3. Does you waiter carry your tray?
4. Is there any tipping in a cafeteria?
5. Are cafeterias usually found only in smaller towns?

Exercise B: Make sentences following the example.

Ex: cafeteria / everyone / waiter
In a cafeteria everyone is really his own waiter.

1. every item / choose / want
2. choose / what / want
3. someone / bill / check
4. carry / tray / empty
5. check / pay / eating

READING

Read the Text:

In some of the busier restaurants there may be a man or lady who will meet you at the door; find you a table, and set you. If there is no such person, simply go in and find your own table. The waiter or waitress will bring a menu and probably a glass of water and leave your table to let you decide what you want to have. If she doesn't bring a menu, you may ask for one: "May I see a menu, please?" Decide what you are going to eat and give the waitress your order when she returns. If you don't know what something on the menu is, ask her to explain it to you; "Could you please tell me what this is (pointing to it on the menu)?" Or if you don't know what to have, you can ask her to suggest something: "What's good today?" or "What would you suggest today?"

When you have decided on you order tell her and she will bring it to you. If she returns to take your order and you have not yet decided, you may ask for more time: "I'd like a little more time, please" or "I haven't quite decided yet." If a man and lady are eating together, the man should ask the lady what she wants and give both order to the waitress.

Exercise A: Indicate whether each of the following statements is true of false by writing the letter T or F in the space provided.

—1. In busier restaurants, a man or lady may meet you at the door.
—2. The waiter or waitress will bring a menu.
—3. If you don't know what something on the menu is, ask her to explain it to you.
—4. When you have decided on you order tell her and she will bring it to you.
—5. If a man and lady are eating together, the man should not ask the lady what she wants and give both orders to the waitress.

Exercise B: Give a brief explanation of some general eating customs and manners in Korea.

Lesson 18

FRUIT

1. Useful Words and Idioms

apiece
to be fresh
to deliver
orchard
to prune / trim
fertilizer / soil
citrus fruits
vitamin
to jell
to furnish
a basket of
How much?
What kind?
to prevent from-ing
by weight
to be present in
to be located on
to enjoy-ing
to belong to
to be made into

2. Common expressions

persimmon
orange / tangerine
strawberry
lemon
mango
melon
chestnut
fig
pomegrante
cherry
plum
walnut
to look damaged
riple
fleshy
to look good
a bunch of grapes

DIALOGUE

Read the Text:

1. A: I want a basket of fruit.
   B: What kind?
   A: Several kinds mixed.
   B: How about these oranges and bananas?
   A: I also want some pineapples.
   B: Will there be anything else?
   A: How much are the apples over there?
   B: Ten cents apiece.
   A: Give me some.
   B: All right. Thank you.
2. A: Show me some melons, please.
   B: Some arrived this morning.
   A: I hope they're fresh.
   B: Very fresh.
   A: How much, please.
   B: Five cents apiece.
   A: Give me five. Will you deliver them to my home?
   B; I'll dispatch them right now.

Exercise A: Restate your part of the conversation from the text.

1. I want a basket of fruit.
2. I also want some pineapples.
3. How much are the apples over there?
4. Show me some.
5. Will you deliver them to my home?

Exercise B: Fill in the blanks.

1. In botany, the term fruit applies to the (   ) of any plant.
2. (   ) to large bodies of water is an advantage in fruit growing.
3. Orchards are often located on slops to prevent (   ) from setting among the trees.
4. Fruit trees should be pruned and trimmed to (   ) their growing.
5. Extreme care is necessary to (   ) bruising the fruits.

COMPOSITION

Read the Text:

Most of the four and a half million aces of orchards in the United States are located on the coasts or near the Great Lakes. Nearness to large bodies of water is an advantage in fruit growing since the water abrupt changes in the temperature of the air.

The springs remain cool thus preventing frost damage from premature blossoming.

The fall ripening period is prolonged and the danger of frost damage to the ripening fruit is reduced. Orchard soils vary widely in composition but almost all are deep and well drained. Few fruit trees are able to survive where the soil is too wet. Orchards are also often located on slopes to prevent cold air from settling among the trees and to encourage air circulation that helps prevent the growth of fungus.

Exercise A: Answer the questions 1 to 5 in complete sentences.

1. What is this text written about?
2. Where are most of the four and a half million acres of orchards located in the United States?
3. How do the springs prevent frost damage from premature blossoming?
4. Where can few fruit trees survive?
5. Why are orchards often located on slopes?

Exercise B: Make sentences following the example.

Ex: nearness / bodies / advantage / fruit growing
Nearness to large bodies of water is an advantage in fruit growing

1. water / modifies / temperature
2. cool / preventing / damage
3. damage / ripening / reduced
4. soils / widely / composition
5. few / are able to / survive / where

READING

Read the Text:

People usually think of peaches, apples, bananas or some berry they particularly enjoy eating when they think of the term fruit. These are some of the delicious fruits found in our daily diet.

In botany, the term fruit applies to th seed of any plant, and all the parts that cover the seed. Thus, fruits can come from the trees, bushes or any plant that produces seed. What we commonly call fruits are more properly the fleshy fruits. Such fruits are important as foods all over the would. They are raised in all the tropical and temperate climates in an endless variety of colors, shapes and sizes.

Among the outstanding fleshy fruits of the would are apples, peaches, pears, melons, grapefruits, lemons, oranges, bananas, figs, cherries, dates, plums and berries. They furnish vitamins, acids and sugar needed by the body, and they are also natural tonics as a mild laxative. The raising of fruits is an important industry in many countries.

Fruits that do not belong to the class of the fleshy fruits are called dry fruits. Examples of these include cereal grains, nuts, peas and beans. Nearly all fleshy fruits can be eaten both raw and cooked. Most of them may be made into jams, jellies, marmalades and butters. The whole fruit may be canned, dried, preserved, or quick-frozen. Some fruits are used to make delicious juices.

Exercise A: Indicate whether each of the following statements is true or false by writing the letter T or F in the space provided.

—1. Potatoes are one of the delicious fruits found in our daily diet.

—2. Fruits can come from trees, bushes, or any plant that produces seed.

—3. What we commonly call fruits are more properly the fleshy fruits.

—4. The raising of fruits is an important industry.

—5. Fruits that belong to the class of the fleshy fruits are called dry apples.

Exercise B: Name ten of your favorite fruits.

GEOGRAPHY

1. Useful Words and Idioms

Region	to visit / call
mainland	as much as possible
to cross	from A to B
to be located	north / south / west / east
continent	to be composed of
ocean / sea	to stretch
to extend	to get the impression that
to cover	in the direction of
direction	

2. Common Expressions

(State)	(Popular Name)	(Capital)
Alabama	Cotton State	Montgomery
Alaska	The Last Frontier	Juneau
Arizona	Grand Canyon State	Phoenix
Arkansas	Land of Opportunity	Little Rock
California	Golden State	Sacramento
Colorado	Cintennial State	Denver
Connecticut	Constitution(Nutmeg) State	Hartford
Delaware	First(Diamond) State	Dover
Florida	Sunshine State	Tallahassee
Georgia	Empire State of the South	Atlanta
Hawaii	Prairie of the Pacific	Honolulu
Idaho	Gem State	Boise
Illinois	Prairie State	Springfield
Indiana	Hoosier State	ndianapolis
Iowa	Hawkeye State	Des Moines
Kansas	Sunflower State	Topeka

Louisiana	Pelican State	Baton Rouge
Maine	Pine Tree State	Augusta
Maryland	Old Line(Free) State	Annapolis
Massachusetts	Bay State or Old Colony	Boston
Michigan	Wolverine State	Lansing
Minnesota	North Star(Gopher) State	St. paul
Mississippi	Magnolia State	Jackson
Missouri	Show Me State	Jefferson City
Montana	Treasure State	Helena
Nebraska	Cornhusker State	Lincoln
Nevada	Sagebrush(Silver) State	Carson City
New Hampshire	Granite State	Concord
New Jersey	Garden State	Trenton
New Mexico	Land of Enchantment	Santa Fe
New York	Empire State	Albany
North Carolina	Tar Heel(Old North) State	Raleigh
North Dakota	Sioux(Fickertail) State	Bismarck
Ohio	Buckeye state	Columbus
Oklahoma	Sooner State	Oklahoma City
Oregon	Beaver State	Salem
Pennsylvania	Keystone State	Harrisburg
Rhode	Island Little Rhody	Providence
South Carolina	Palmetto State	Columbia
South Dakota	Coyote (Sunshine) State	Pierre
Tennessee	Volunteer State	Nashville
Texas	Lone Star State	Austin
Utah	Beehive State	Salt lake City
Vermont	Green Mountain State	Montpelier
Virginia	Old Dominion	Richmond
Washington	Evergreen State	Olympia
West Virginia	Mountain State	Charleston
Wisconsin	Badger State	Madison
Wyoming	Equality State	Cheyenne

DIALOGUE

Read the Text:

1. A: What places do you want to visit in the United States?
   B: I want to visit New York.
   A: I want to see some National Parks.
   The Grand Canyon first, then Yellowstone.
   B: It's a thousand miles from the Grand Canyon to Yellowstone Park.
   A: How far is it from San Francisco to New York?
   B: It's about three thousand miles, I think. Why?
   A: I want to visit a cousin in New York and a friend in San Francisco While I'm in the States.

2. A: A friend of mine took a trip to California by car.
   B: That's a long trip. How long did it take him?
   A: About six weeks. He wanted to see as much as possible.
   B: What route did he take?
   A: He went to California by the southern route and came back by the northern route.
   B: Where did he cross the Mississippi?
   A: He crossed it the first time at New Orleans.

Exercise A: Restate your part of the conversation from the text.

1. What places do you want to visit in the United States?
2. How far is it from San Francisco to New York?
3. It's about three thousand miles from San Francisco to New York, I think, Why?
4. What route did he take?
5. Where did he cross the Mississippi?

Exercise B: Fill in the blanks.

1. From the East Coast to the West Coast it is about (   ) miles wide.
2. (   ) is the county to the north of the United States.
3. There are (   ) states in the United States today.

4. (　　) is the boundary between Mexico and the United States.
5. The two newest states, (　　) and (　　) are geographically separated from the other 48 states.

COMPOSITION

Read the Text:

The United States, which is located on the continent of North America, is one of the largest countries in the world. It covers more than three million square miles and has a population of about 234 million people. The United States is composed of fifty different states. The largest of these is Alaska. The smallest is Rhode Island.

The capital of the United States is Washington, D.C. North of the United States lies another large country, Canada. The population of Canada is over 25 million people. The Atlantic Ocean is east of the United States. The Pacific Ocean is west of the United States. South of the United States lies the Spanish–American country of Mexico. The population of Mexico is over 55 million people.

Exercise A: Answer the questions 1 to 5 in complete sentences.

1. Where is the United States?
2. How many square miles does it cover?
3. Which country lies north of the United States?
4. Is Pennsylvania the smallest state?
5. Where is the Atlantic Ocean located?

Exercise B: Make sentences following the example.

Ex: covers / square / population
It covers more than three million square miles and has a population of about 234 million people.

1. United States / composed / different
2. largest / states / Alaska
3. capital / United States / Washington
4. population / Canada / 25 million
5. south / lies / Spanish – America / Mexico

READING

Read the Text:

The present mainland of the United States stretches, east to west, from the Atlantic Ocean to the Pacific Ocean. These two great bodies of water seen so clearly to be the "natural" east-west boundaries of the country that one sometimes gets the impression that the United States always existed in its present form. Yet, as we well know, this is not true.

The United States began as a narrow section of territory along the Atlantic coast. Later, with victory in the American Revolution, the boundary was extended as far west as the Mississippi River. This was the first step in the country's growth.

The second great step was the Louisiana Purchase. By that purchase, the country was suddenly doubled in size. The United States now extended well beyond the Mississippi River. The exact western limits of the new territory were not known; the treaty itself was not clear on this pint. But this was not too important. The important fact was that no strong foreign power now held territory to the west of us. The young United States was able to grow in the direction of the distant Pacific.

Exercise A: Indicate whether each of the following statements is true or false by writing the letter T or F in the space provided.

—1. The present mainland of the United States stretches, west to east, from the Pacific Ocean to the Atlantic Ocean.
—2. The United States began as a narrow section of territory along the Pacific coast.
—3. Later, with victory in the American Revolution, the boundary was extended as far west as the Mississippi River.
—4. The first great step was the Louisiana Purchase.
—5. The young United States was able to grow in the direction of the distant Pacific.

Exercise B: Where is your country located?

Lesson 20

SUBWAY

1. Useful Words and Idioms

excavation
token
headline
street traffic
an hour or so
subway underground
cashier cummuter
suburban
flat
freight car

to be bound for
as far as
to pay attention to
to make sure
to be against the law
to keep off
to hold on to
to get on / off
to play a vital part in

2. Common Expressions

booth
fare
turnstile
slot
platform
seat
pole
signs
advertisements
passenger
dandruff
advice
right / wrong

to ride the subway
to stand back of the White Line
to arrive on time

DIALOGUE

Read the Text:

1. A: Where is this subway train bound for?
   B: It is going as far as Incheon.
   A: Will it pass Seoul Station?
   B: Yes, I think so.
   A: How often does the train for Incheon come?
   B: It comes every 15 minutes.
   A: Thank you.

2. A: How far away do you live?
   B: I live just outside the city. I get on the subway at Fourth Street and get off at Twelfth Street. From there I walk to my office.
   A: How long does it take in all to get to your office?
   B: Nearly an hour and a half.
   A: That's pretty long. The subway is awfully crowed in the morning.
   B: Not as crowded as I thought it would be.

Exercise A: Restate your part of the conversation from the text.

1. Where is this subway train bound for?
2. Will it pass Seoul Station?
3. How often does the train for Incheon come?
4. How far away do you live?
5. How long does it take in all to get to your office?

Exercise B: Fill in the blanks.

1. Subways may be constructed by tunneling, or by (   ) an open trench and then covering the excavation.
2. London was the (   ) city to have a subway.
3. You've gotten (   ) at the wrong station.
4. We got (   ) the subway train for Soowon.
5. The subway is (   ) especially in the morning.

COMPOSITION

Read the Text:

I generally go to school by subway. The subway is always crowded and I don't often get a seat. In the subway, on my way to school, I look at the signs on the walls of the car, watch the faces of the other passengers, and read the newspaper headlines over someone's shoulder. It takes me about half an hour to get to school. My first class begins at nine o'clock and my last class ends at three. After school hours, I sometimes go to the Student Center or to a coffee house with my friends for an hour or so. Afterwards I go home.

Exercise A: Answer the questions 1 to 5 in complete sentences.

1. How do you generally go to school?
2. What do you do in the subway?
3. How long does it take you to get to school?
4. What time does your last class end?
5. Where do you sometimes go after school hours?

Exercise B: Make sentences following the example.

Ex: generally / go / subway
I generally go to school by subway.

1. subway / crowded / don't / seat
2. look at / sing / walls
3. It / me / get to
4. first class / begin / end
5. I / go / my friends

READING

Read the Text:

SUBWAY, an underground railway. Subways relieve street-traffic congestion and permit the movement of passengers, and in some cities, of freight, at higher speeds than are possible on the streets. Subways are also free of the ugliness and noise characteristic of elevated railways.

Subways may be constructed by tunneling, or by digging an open trench and then covering the excavation. They are provided with ventilating fans, usually of a type that be operated either to draw fresh air in or blow foul air out.

London was the first city to have a subway. Its first "tube" opened in 1863. Most of the world's leading cities now have subways, including New York City, Tokyo, Chicago, Paris, Barcelona, Calcutta, Rome, Buenos Aires, Stockholm, Copenhagen, Berlin, Hamburg and Sydney.

Electricity plays a vital part in modern systems of rail transportation. In many crowed cities throughout the world electrically powered streetcars, subway trains and elevated railways carry billions of passengers every year. Swift electric trains bring commuters from their suburban homes to the offices and shops of the city. Over mountains and across flat plains, powerful locomotives, driven by electric or diesel-electric motors, pull long strings of passenger and freight cars.

Exercise A: Indicate whether each of the following statements is true or false by writing the letter T or F in the space provided.

—1. Subways are also free of the ugliness and noise characteristic of elevated railways.

—2. Subways may be constructed by tunneling, or by digging an open trench and then covering the excavation.

—3. The world's leading cities now have subways.

—4. Electricity plays a common part in modern systems of rail transportation.

—5. Swift electric trains bring commuters from their suburban homes to the offices and shops of the city.

Exercise B: Briefly explain how to ride the subway in Seoul.

Lesson 21

BUS

1. Useful Words and Idioms

bus stop / station
to transfer
city / local / inter-city bus
to serve
to carry
passenger
long distance run
transfer slip
baggage racks
express / local train
to figure out
to get off / on
to be eager to
to change buses
a large number of
to take about
by bus / train
along the way
to make one's trip

2. Common Expressions

oneway
ticket
terminal
tourist's round trip
a tour around the city
to pay the guide
to show around
sightseeing bus
to take a trip
by hired bus
to take the bus to (Brooklyn)
to be bound for (Miami)
to g as far as (Incheon)
What's the fare to(Hilton)?

DIALOGUE

Read the Text:

1. A: I can't figure out this bus route.
   B: It's going to Central Park.
   A: Does this bus stop at the Union Hotel?
   B: You've gotten on the wrong bus.
   A: Where do I change buses?
   B: You can change buses at this stop.

2. A: Dose this bus go all the way to the City Hall, or do I have to transfer?
   B: No, you'll have to transfer.
   A: Where do I change buses, and what bus do I catch?
   B: You'll have to get off at 5th ave and Walnut and catch the Fairview bus going north.
   A: Would you give me a transfer slip, please?
   B: Sure. Here.
   A: Thanks. And would you please tell me when we get there?
   B: Sure.

Exercise A: Restate your part of the conversation from the text.

1. Does this bus stop at the Union Hotel?
2. Where do I change buses?
3. Does this bus go all the way to the City Hall?
4. What bus do I catch?
5. Would you give me a transfer slip, please?

Exercise B: Fill in the blanks.

1. (   ) is the fare?
2. (   ) buses are slower and stop in every little town they go through.
3. The (   ) will show you what towns you will pass through.
4. (   ) are necessary on a few buses.
5. Do I get (   ) here?

COMPOSITION

Read the Text:

Buses in the United States. There are three general types of buses in use in the United States today – city or local, inter-city, and school. City buses are powered by diesel fuel, kerosene, gasoline, or electricity. Though designed for comfort, such buses are also built to carry a large number of passengers, both seated and standing.

There are about 1,600 local bus companies, operating some 52,000 buses and carrying nearly six billion passengers annually. Inter-city buses, built for long-distance runs and fast highway speeds, are usually powered by diesel or gasoline motors.

Heavy and powerful, they include such comport features as air conditioning, reclining seats, interior baggage racks, glare-proof windows, music and toilets. A few also provide light lunches. The 1,700 intercity bus companies operate about 25,000 buses and carr about 550,000,000 passengers a year.

School buses are usually lighter and carry fewer passengers than either the city or intercity buses. There are nearly 160,000 school buses in operation, many in rural districts where the school may serve a wide area. About eleven million school children, more than a third of the total, daily use bus transportation for school.

Exercise A: Answer the questions 1 to 5 in complete sentences.

1. What are city buses powered by?
2. How many local bus companies are there?
3. What are inter-city buses usually powered by?
4. Are there nearly 52,000 school buses in operation?
5. How many children daily use bus transportation for school?

Exercise B: Make sentences following the example.

Ex: three / buses / U. S. / today
There are three general types of buses in use in the U.S. today.

1 . city / powered / electricity
2. buses / planned / passengers
3. inter-city / powered / motors
4. a few / provide / lunches
5. school / passengers / either

READING

Read the Text:

The bus is the most inexpensive means of travel in America, but it is also the slowest. For example, whereas it takes about ten hours to fly from San Francisco to New York and about forty hours by train, it takes about seventy-five hours by bus. This, of course, can make your trip more tiresome, but it costs only about half as much to go by bus as it does to go by train. The cost of traveling by bus is about 2 $\frac{1}{2}$ cents per mile.

Trains and buses are of two types — "express" and "local." "Express" means that it is a faster train or bus doesn't stop in every little town along the way. The "local" buses and trains are slower and stop in every little town they go through, or express, and of possible, take only the express. Of course if you are going to a town at which the express doesn't stop, it will be necessary to take the local. Sometimes express trains are called "limited" trains.

Exercise A: Indicate whether each of the following statements is true or false by writing the letter T or F in the space provided.

—1. The bus is the most expensive means of travel in America.
—2. It takes about ten hours to fly from San Francisco to New York and about seventy-five hours by bus.
—3. Buses stop every two or three hours for the passengers to eat and go to the toilet.
—4. "Express" means that it is a faster train or bus and stops in every little town along the way.
—5. Sometimes express trains are called "limited" trains.

Exercise B: How many kinds of buses are there in your country?

Lesson 22

SIGHTSEEING

1. Useful Words and Idioms

pamphlet / booklet
information
to recommend
to attend
landscape / spectacle
bus line
monument
to publicize
route
tourist / traveller
to be worth one's while
to be interested in
to feel like –ing
in advance
on the other side
in addition to
for the first time
to take a trip
to specialize in
throughout the year

2. Common Expressions

remains
gondola
souvenir
statue
historic relics
fountain
guide fee
tourist agent
itinerary
cathedral
admission fee
scenic region
for a change
a tour around the city
to show around
round trip
amusement district
celadon

DIALOGUE

Read the Text:

1. A: Where may I have some information about city tours?
   B: We have some pamphlets to explain the tours available here.
   A: Which interesting sights would you recommend?
   B: You mustn't miss seeing Disneyland.
   A: How about visiting Yellowstone?
   B: You'd find it well worth your while.
   A: Have you been there before?
   B: Of course. The geysers're fascinating to see.
   A: What's the best way to enjoy all of them?
   B: I recommend taking a tour bus.
2. A: I'm quite interested in folk art.
   B: Let's go to the Korean Folk Village.
   A: It's very nice of you to go with me.
   B: I'd like you to sample some folk village dong-dong-ju. That's a special rice wine.
   A: I feel like having a drink.
   B: I'll join you.

Exercise A: Restate your part of the conversation from the text.

1. Where may I have some information about city tours?
2. Which interesting sights would recommend?
3. How about visiting Yellowstone?
4. Have you been there before?
5. I'm quite interested in folk art.

Exercise B: Fill in the blanks.

1. I'm going to take ( ) Hawaii.
2. Do I pay the fare ( ) advance?
3. Shall we ( ) over and get something to drink?
4. Do you have change ( ) a dollar?
5. You'd better check ( ) the Lost and Found.

COMPOSITION

Read the Text:

Colorado National Monument is an area of fantastically eroded and vividly colored highlands. Its sheer-walled canyons, towering monoliths, stratified ramparts and fluted columns combine to present a spectacle of imposing grandeur. The Uncompahgre Highlands has been worn away by erosion over millions of years and this slow cutting away of the sediments left today's rugged landscape, as well as exposing petrified wood and dinosaur bones.

There is also evidence that prehistoric Indians lived in the canyons. Later, the Ute Indians made their homes in the area. Spanish explorers passed this way for first time in August, 1776. In the 1830's, French trappers established a supply and trading post near present-day Delta, about 60 miles south of Colorado National Monument. Late in the 19th century John Otto settled in Monument Canyon, and over the succeeding years built many roads and trails throughout what is now the National Monument. After the turn of th century, Otto began to publicize the spectacular scenery of the area through numerous letters to friends and various officials. Otto's long campaign was successful; on May 24, 1911, President Taft proclaimed the establishment of the Colorado National Monument, and named John Otto as its custodian.

Exercise A: Answer the questions 1 to 5 in complete sentences.

1. What is an area of fantastically eroded and vividly colored highlands?
2. What place has been worn away by erosion over millions of years?
3. Who passed this way for the first time in August, 1776?
4. When did John Otto settle in Monument Canyon?
5. What did President Taft proclaim on May 24, 1911?

Exercise B: Make the sentences following the example.

Ex: Colorado / area / eroded
Colorado National Monument is an area of fantastically eroded and vividly colored highlands.

1. Uncompahgre Highlands / worn / erosion
2. Ute Indian / homes / area
3. Spanish / passed / 1776
4. 1830's / French / established
5. publicize / scenery / officials

READING

Read the Text:

More ambitious vacationers take extensive automobile trips through different sections of the country. They visit such historic places as Williamsburg, Virginia (a seventeenth-century colonial town), Abraham Lincoln's birthplace in Kentucky, the French Quarter in New Orleans, and old Spanish missions in the Southwest. Or they visit national parks like Yellowstone and the Grand Canyon in the Rocky Mountains and the Everglades in Florida. Other families prefer to spend their vacations visiting large cities.

The United States Capitol, the Empire State Building, and the Golden Gate Bridge attract thousands of tourists. In addition to the sightseeing they do, tourists like to attend the plays, the concerts, the stage shows and other attractions of the big cities. They enjoy the restaurants, the crowds and the variety of life.

Washington and New York are crowded with teenagers every spring as organized groups of high school pupils go sightseeing. Most cities have bus lines specializing in sightseeing, with drivers who describe the interesting attractions along the route. Tourist attractions also have regularly scheduled tours throughout the year.

Exercise A: Indicate whether each of the following statements is true or false by writing the letter T or F in the space provided.

—1. More ambitious vacationers take extensive automobile trips through different sections of the country. Grand Canyon in Florida.

—3. Other families prefer to spend their vacations visiting countryside.

—4. In addition to the sightseeing they do, tourists like to attend the plays, the concerts, the stage shows and other attractions of the big cities.

—5. Washington and New York are not crowded with teenagers every spring.

Exercise B: Could you suggest some interesting places to visit in Korea?

20
32
33
80

Lesson 23

AIRPORT

1. Useful Words and Idioms

ticket
passport
visa
customs
statistics
means
appetite
schedule
skyline
sky scraper
announcement
life raft
isolated
emergency

to be due
to get nervous
to be tied up
to reach / arrive at(in)
to land at
to stare at
to pack / unpack
to impress
to become good friends

2. Common Expressions

domestic flights
overseas flights
aisle seat
immunization certificate
duty-free shop
take-off
vacant
occupied
lavatory
baggage claim
inclement weather

to have refreshment
to pay the duty
to be due
to cancel one's reservation
to make reservation
to pass the custom house
to impose a duty

DIALOGUE

Read the Text:

1. A: Show me your ticket and passport, please.
   B: Certainly. Here they are. I have no visa.
   I'm here for an over-night stay only.
   A: O.K. You can stay here 72 hours.
   B: Where should I go from here now?
   A: Take your baggage with you and go to customs.

2. A: Good morning. Alpha Airlines.
   B: Reservations, please.
   A: Reservations. May I hope you?
   B: Yes, I want to make reservations to Atlanta.
   A: I can give you something on Flight 549.
   It is leaving at 4:45 p.m.
   B: Yes, I'll do that.
   A: May I have your name, please?
   B: Nicholas Bateman.
   A: Thanks very much, sir. And thank you for calling Alpha.

Exercise A: Restate your part of the conversation from the text.

1. Show me your ticket and passport, please.
2. O.K. You can stay here 72 hours.
3. Good morning. Alpha Airlines.
4. Reservations. May I help you?
5. I can give you something on Flight 549.
   It is leaving at 4:45 p. m.

Exercise B: Fill in the blanks.

1. I tried to call you but the line was ( ).
2. This flight is due ( ) 9: 55.
3. He is ( ) flight 549.
4. I want to make ( ) for a party of four.
5. What do I need to travel ( ) plane?

COMPOSITION

Read the Text:

I arrived in the United States on February 6, 1966, but I remember my first day here very clearly. My friend was waiting for me when my plane landed at Kennedy Airport at three o'clock in the afternoon. The weather was very cold and it was snowing, but I was too excited to mind. From the airport, my friend and I took a taxi to my hotel. On the way, I saw the skyline of Manhattan for the first time and I stared in astonishment at the famous skyscrapers and their man-made beauty. My friend helped me unpack at the hotel and then left me because he had to go back to work. He promised to return the next day.

Exercise A: Answer the questions 1 to 5 in complete sentences.

1. When did you arrive in the United States?
2. How did you come?
3. Where did your plane land?
4. What was the weather like?
5. What did you see on the way to your hotel?

Exercise B: Make sentences following the example.

Ex: remember / first day / clearly
I remember my first day here very clearly.

1. I / arrive / the United States
2. I / excited / mind
3. take / taxi / hotel.
4. friend / me / unpack
5. He / promise / return

READING

Read the Text:

Soon the announcement comes that passengers on my flight, Flight 707 for Miami, Florid, should assemble at Gate 8. There we all gather, a rather sad and worried-looking lot. I look over the group to see what kind of people I am to spend my final hours with. After all, we may come down on some isolated mountain spot or we may spend days floating around the ocean on life rafts. There doesn't seem to be anyone in the group I would like to share either of thee experiences with. True, there is a very attractive young blonde, sitting not far away. It might not be too painful spending a few hours on the same life raft with her.

I could impress her with my great strength and courage in such an emergency — and later we might become good friends. But what am I thinking about? I am a man almost fifty years old and she is a girl of twenty-five. What would really happen is this: On the life raft she would take one look at me and the push me overboard to make room for the handsome young fellow siting opposite her and already casing amorous glances in her direction.

Exercise A: Indicate whether each of he following statements is true or false by writing the letter T or F in the space provided.

—1. Flight 707 for Miami, Florida, should assemble at Gate 8.
—2. There we all gather, a father happy and pleased-looking lot.
—3. We must come sown on some isolated mountain spot and spend days floating around the ocean on life rafts.
—4. It might not be too painful spending a few hours on the same life raft with her.
—5. I am a man almost fifty years old and she is a girl of twenty-five.

Exercise B: How do you spend your time while waiting for the plane to leave?

Lesson 24

AIR TRAVELING

1. Useful Words and Idioms

one-way / single ticket
to reconfirm
flight number
reservation
baggage / luggage
to check
to board
stewardess
passenger
convenient
emergency
suitcase / trunk
to take a trip
to feel airsick
to travel by plane
to take it easy
to relax
to be arranged for
to take off
to pick up
to look forward to
to look up

2. Common Expressions

airline
departure time
air travel
travel agent
chartered flight
non-stop
stop-over
delays
round trip
screw
life vest
When do we get there?
Fasten your seat belt
relaxed
earache
tired
bored
airsick

DIALOGUE

Read the Tex:

1. A: I'd like to fly to Los Angeles next Friday.
   B: You can reserve a seat leaving for Los Angeles nest Friday.
   A: How much is a round-trip ticket?
   B: Same as two one-way tickets.
   A: When will it arrive in Los Angeles?
   B: A little after nine a.m. the next day.
   Shall I make a reservation for you now?
   A: Yes, I'd appreciate it if you would.

2. A: Ticket and passport, please.
   B: Certainly. Here you are.
   A: You're going all the way to New York?
   B: Yes, that's right. Can you check my baggage straight through?
   A: You have just these two pieces?
   B: Yes, but I don't want to check the briefcase.
   A: I'll have to weight it anyway. That takes care of everything.
   B: Thank you.

Exercise A: Restate your part of the conversation from the text.

1. I'd like to fly to Los Angeles nest Friday.
2. How much is a round-trip ticket?
3. When will it arrive in Los Angeles?
4. Ticket and passport, please.
5. You're going all the way to New York?

Exercise B: Fill in the blanks.

1. What time dose your next plane leave ( ) Kansas City?
2. Do I have to change ( ) in Denver?
3. Are there any ( ) on the way?
4. What time are we ( ) into New Orleans.
5. ( )'s the fare to Detroit?

COMPOSITION

Read the Text:

Last summer, I took my first airplane flight from London to New York. I boarded the plane at Croydon Airfield and, from that moment on, my life was arranged for me on the trip. First, I was directed to my seat by the stewardess. Then, when the plane was ready to take off, the other passengers and I were told to fasten our seat belts, A few minutes after take–off, magazines and newspapers were passed out (distributed). Because my ears hurt, I was given some gum to chew. Next, we were given instructions on what to do in case of an emergency. We were given earphones to listen to music and told that a move would be shown after dinner, Before dinner, we were asked if we wanted a cocktail. Dinner was served on a tray, but it was attractive and delicious. We were permitted to have a refill on any beverage. After dinner, we were shown a new Hollywood movie. When I felt cold, I was given a blanket and when I felt airsick, I was given a paper bag. Everything was done for the comfort of the passengers. When the plane landed, I was almost sorry to get off and had to start doing things for myself again.

Exercise A: Answer the questions 1 to 5 in complete sentences.

1. When did you take your first airplane flight?
2. Where did you board the plane?
3. Who directed you to your seat?
4. What were you asked before dinner?
5. Why were you sorry when the plane landed?

Exercise B: Make sentences following the example.

Ex: life / arranged / trip
My life was arranged for me on the trip.

1. told / fasten / belts
2. given / gum / chew
3. diner / served / attractive
4. permitted / refill / beverage
5. everything / comfort / passengers

READING

Read the Text:

There are many advantages to traveling by air even though it is the most expensive means of traveling. It is by far the fastest means of travel and the most comfortable and convenient. Meals are served on the plane at no extra cost. There is no tipping on th e plane.

You can only take about 20 kilograms of luggage on the plane, so if you have other suitcases or trunks, you will have to send them by railway express. Or if you are in no hurry for them, you could send them by railway freight which is slower but less expensive. All you have to do is phone the Express or Freight office, tell them you have some suitcases and trunks to send, and give them your address. Then they will send a truck to your address to pick them up and take them to the railway express or freight station.

You need a reservation on almost all planes, so ask for one at the time you buy your ticket. Almost all airway lines have a ticket reservation since the airport is usually located outside of the city. You can learn the address of the downtown ticket office by looking it up in the phone book.

Exercise A: Indicate whether each of the following statements is true or false by writing the letter T or F in the space provided.

—1. There are many advantages to traveling by air because it is the most expensive means of traveling.

—2. Meals are served on the plane at no extra cost.

—3. You can only take about 20 kilograms of luggage on the plane, so if you have other suitcases or trunks, you will have to send them by railway express.

—4. You need a reservation on almost all planes, so ask for one at the time you buy your ticket.

—5. You can learn the address of the downtown ticket office by looking it up in the reservation book.

Exercise B: How many advantage are there to traveling by air?

Lesson 25

HOTEL

1. Useful Words and Idioms

single / double room
available
to lodge
porter
luxurious
accommodation
summer resort
conveniences
motel / hotel

to range from A to B
in contrast
on vacation
to make up
to check in / out
in front of
for a brief stay
to get into
to be located on / in
to be looking for

2. Common Expressions

suitcase
luggage
front desk
valuables
bellboy / bellhop
key
elevator
ground floor / main floor
second floor
maid / chambermaid
vacant

to make one's home in a hotel
to put at a hotel
to stay at a hotel
to keep / run a hotel
to keep the change
to fill in the form
to make (a) reservation
to post a letter

DIALOGUE

Read the Text:

1. A: Hello. Biltmore Hotel.
   B: Hello, do you have any single rooms available?
   A: Yes, we do have a few.
   B: What price rooms do you have?
   A: We have one for $4.00 with bath.
   B: Fine. Would you save it for me? My name is Kim.
   A: Yes, we will.
   B: I'll be right over.
   A: Thank you very much. Good-bye.

2. A: I'm checking out. Will you make out my bill?
   B: Yes, sir. Your bill comes to 55 dollars.
   A: Can you send up a porter for my baggage?
   B: Certainly, sir.

Exercise A: Restate your part of the conversation from the text.

1. Hello, do you have any single rooms available?
2. What price rooms do you have?
3. Fine. Would you save it for me? My name is Kim.
4. I'm checking out. Will you make out my bill?
5. Can you send up a porter for my baggage?

Exercise B: Fill in the blanks.

1. Hello. I have a (   ) for a single room.
2. In American hotels, all meals, phone calls and other services are not included in the (   ).
3. Rooms for one person only are called (   ) rooms.
4. You should always keep your hotel room door (   ).
5. You will be expected to (   ) bellhops for all their service.

COMPOSITION

Read the Text:

Hotels are of five main types — commercial (transient), residential, resort, club and motel. Commercial hotels, the largest group, cater to travelers seeking a room for a brief stay. In contrast, residential hotels usually accommodate people for periods of a few months to many years. Both operate all year around. Resort hotels, generally operate at certain seasons, provided lodgings and recreation for people on vacation. Club hotels, which provide both lodging and food, usually cater to members only. In size, hotels range from two — or three— story structures to towering buildings with a thousand or more rooms. Several hotels may be owned and operated by a single cooperation and make up a hotel chain.

Exercise A: Answer the questions 1 to 5 in complete sentences.

1. How many main types of hotels are there?
2. Describe the residential hotels.
3. When are resort hotels operated?
4. What kind of hotel usually caters to members only?
5. What may several hotels make up?

Exercise B: Make sentences following the example.

Ex: hotels / five / types
Hotels are of five main types.

1. commercial / cater / travelers
2. resort / operated / certain
3. resort / provide / recreation
4. club / provide / lodging
5. several / owned / hotel chain

READING

Read the Text:

Sunnybrook, Florida is a delightful summer resort by the ocean. It's a very small place with only a few homes and one small hotel. But both the homes and the hotel are very luxurious. Only rich elderly people own the houses and stay at the hotel.

One day a car stopped in front of the hotel and a handsome fellow got out. He walked into the lobby of the hotel, stopped and looked around. He then approached the reception desk and rang the bell for the receptionist. An elderly gentleman came to the desk and asked, "What can I do for you, son?" The young man answered, "I'm looking for Mr. Rivers, my uncle. Is he here?" The old man answer, "He was here but he left for New York this morning." "Oh, no!" said the young man. "His secretary told me that he was going to stay here for another week!" The old man said, "Yes, that's true, but early this morning, he received a telephone call and had to return to New York as soon as possible. You know – important business." The young man said angrily, "I sent him a letter last week. He knew I was coning. Well, there's nothing I can do now. Thank you anyway."

The young man left the hotel, got into his car and drove off. The receptionist then called, "Oh, Mr. Rivers! Come down now! He's left."

Mr. Rivers came downstairs. "Thank you very much." He said. And he started laughing. "That young nephew of mine is always asking for money, but this time I fooled him."

Exercise A: Indicate whether each of the following statements is true or false by writing the letter T or F in the space provided.

—1. Sunnybrook, Florida si a delightful summer resort by the ocean.

—2. One day a car stooped in front of the hotel and a handsome fellow got out.

—3. A handsome fellow came to the desk and asked, "What can I do for you, son?"

—4. The old man said angrily, "I sent him a letter last week. He knew I was coming."

—5. Mr. Rivers came downstairs. "Thank you very much," he said. And he started laughing.

Exercise B: When you leave the hotel to go shopping, etc., whom would you leave your key at the desk with?

Lesson 26

TELEVISION

1. Useful Words and Idioms

television / TV
program
moderation
communication
appearance
station
entertainment
variety show
quality
locally / nationally
popular

to have influence on / upon
to be reported to
to turn on / off
to keep in touch with
to prefer to
to have an effect on
to watch television
to exist as
to strive to

2. Common Expressions

home comedy
talk show
to turn up / down
What's on TV / the program / channel 9 now?
They are presenting / televizing a Western picture now.
popular
to miss
to watch on TV

DIALOGUE

Read the Text:

1. A: Is there anything good on TV tonight?
   B: I don't know. Let's turn it on and see.
   A: O.K. Which program is showing?
   B: That seems to be a drama. Try another station.
   A: All right. I'll turn to another station.
   B: That looks like some kind of musical program. Isn't there anything funny showing?

2. A: My brother turns on the TV and keeps watching until dinner time.
   B: Until dinner time! That's a little better than my sister. She watches it throughout dinner.
   A: It's really hard to use it in moderation. What are her favorite programs?
   B: Mainly cartoons. How about your brother's?

Exercise A: Restate your part of the conversation from the text.

1. Is there anything good on TV tonight?
2. O.K. Which program is showing?
3. That seems to be a drama. Try another station.
4. It's really hard to use it in moderation.
   What are her favorite programs?
5. Mainly cartoons. How about your brother's?

Exercise B: Fill in the blanks.

1. With the advent of (　) man gained the opportunity to watch events taking place in distant locations.
2. (　) television is no different in principle from black.
3. The (　) of a sending station must be mounted high.
4. Many thousands of college students are instructed by (　) as a supplement to regular classes.
5. Every year American industry spends millions of dollars in (　).

COMPOSITION

Read the Text:

Most U.S. family have television in their homes. It has become popular during the last fifteen years. Radio used to be the most popular home entertainment. Now most people like to watch television.

We prefer to both see and hear the programs. We enjoy many of programs. We see comedies, dramas, musicals and variety shows. There are also news and weather reports.

There are three big television companies in the United States. They have programs in all parts of the country. People all over United States can see the same programs. There are some small company.

Exercise A: Answer the questions 1 to 5 in complete sentences.

1. How many families have television in their homes?
2. What did radio use to be?
3. How many programs are there? What kinds?
4. Are there big television companies in the U.S.?
5. Can people all over the States see the same programs?

Exercise B: Make sentences following the example.

Ex: become / during / fifteen
It has become popular during the last fifteen years.

1. now / like / watch
2. prefer / both / programs
3. enjoy / kinds / programs
4. people / U.S. / some programs
5. there / smaller / are

READING

Read the Text:

Television exists as a function of society it serves, and like society it is imperfect. The television networks, according to their representatives, strive conscientiously to improve the quality, diversity and balance of their programs. Because there is a comedy show, there is also an opera program. Because there is a Western adventure series, there also are televised programs in physics, chemistry, literature and other educational features. Because there are popular singers and variety shows, there is a series of conversations with the wise men of our time.

The financial support which advertisers give to the big, popular shows for the big audiences makes the "specialized" shows possible. Television's role in education has won acclaim in many quarters.

The first country-wide educational television project was "Continental Classroom", begun in 1958. It presented two-semester, college-level courses in physics, chemistry, mathematics, and American government. It brought to viewers outstanding teachers and, as guest lecturers, many distinguished figures including Nobel prize winners. Similar courses and related educational programing are presented locally and nationally by stations and networks and by an educational network that serves those stations devoted exclusively to educational broadcasting.

Exercise A: Indicate whether each of the following statements is true or false by writing the letter T or F in the provided.

—1. Television exists as a function of the society it serves, and like society it is imperfect.

—2. Because there is a comedy show, there is a Western adventure series.

—3. Television's role education has won acclaim in many quarters.

—4. The first country-wide educational television project was "American Classroom" begun in 1958.

—5. It brought to viewers outstanding teachers and many distinguished figures including Nobel prize winners.

Exercise B: Which do you like better, radio programs or television programs?

Lesson 27

CAMERA

1. Useful Words and Idioms

to focus
to develop
to print
to enlarge
photography
to portray
telescope
inventor
motion-picture camera
knob
to fix the camera
to turn out
the day after tomorrow
the day before yesterday
to come out
to become important
to condense into
in miniature
by oneself
to be equipped with

2. Common Expressions

reel
thermometer
exposure
telephoto lens
tripod
shutter to
safety filter
negative
printing paper
grain paper
timer
finder
a roll of film
enlarging
developing
to operate
to be guaranteed
to take pictures
to snap

DIALOGUE

Read the Text:

1. A: A time day for taking picture!
   B: Here's a good place for a picture.
   A: Just stand there. I'll fix the camera.
   B: Could you take our picture with this camera?
   C: Certainly. can you tell me how to use it?
   A: All you have to do is to focus it. And press this button.
   C: Say cheese. All right.
   A: How will the photo turn out?
   B: I hope it'll come out good.
   C: I'm sure it will.
2. A: I want this color film developed, printed and enlarged.
   B: What kind of paper shall I use?
   A: Glossy paper, please. When can I have them?
   B: Your order will be ready the day after tomorrow.
   A: I need a roll of Kodak color film.
   B: Here it is, sir.

Exercise A: Restate your part of the conversation from the text.

1. What a fine day it is for taking pictures!
2. Could you take our picture with this camera?
3. How will the photo turn out?
4. What kind of paper shall I use?
5. When can I have them?

Exercise B: Fill in the blanks.

1. Do you have a (　　) of operating instructions?
2. I want this film made (　　) slides.
3. I'd like to learn how to (　　) this camera.
4. Are you going to (　　) our pictures?
5. The picture came (　　) nicely.

COMPOSITION

Read the Text:

Thomas Edison was a great American inventor. He was born in Ohio in 1847. As a child, he wasn't very interested in school. He went to school for only three months. He received most of his education from his mother and from reading books by himself.

Edison invented the phonograph in 1877. But his most successful invention was the electric light. His last major invention was the motion picture camera and projector. He invented them in 1891.

The world owes Edison a great deal. Today our lives are far more comfortable because of his great inventions.

Exercise A: Answer the questions 1 to 5 in complete sentences.

1. Was Thomas Edison a great American architect?
2. When was he born?
3. How did he get his education?
4. What did he invent in 1877?
5. What was his last major invention?

Exercise B: Make the sentences following the example.

Ex: Thomas Edison / great / inventor
Thomas Edison was a great American inventor.

1. went / school / months
2. received / education / mother
3. invented / phonograph / 1877
4. world / owes / deal
5. lives / comfortable / inventions

READING

Read the Text:

Motion-picture cameras are made in 8-mm and 16-mm sizes for general use, and in 35-mm size for projection on theater screens. Several of these cameras have electronic synchronized controls which operate with tape recorders to record sound. Some amateur-type cameras have there lenses for normal, wide-angle, and telephoto purposes. Professional models have many different lenses for obtaining a wide variety of effects and are equipped to record sound directly on the film. Camera manufacturers, attempting to simplify picture taking, have devised auto-lens cameras in which an electric eye inside the view finder controls the lens iris.

The electronic eye is a small piece of selenium oxide which generates a tiny electric current when exposed to light. This current operates the iris, adjusting the size of the opening according to the amount of available light. There are also semiautomatic cameras in which the electric eye is not connected directly to the iris. By turning a knob, two arrows in a window, one from the electric eye, the other form the iris, are brought into alignment. Still other cameras have built-in exposure meters.

The photographer sets the lens opening to correspond with the amount of light registered on the meter. Some motion-picture cameras are equipped with the electric eye, some are semiautomatic, and some have built-in light meters.

Exercise A: Indicate whether each of the following statements is rue or false by writing the letter T or F in the space provided.

—1. Motion picture cameras are made in 35-mm sizes for general use.

—2. Some amateur-type cameras have three lenses for normal wide-angle and telephoto purposes.

—3. The electric eye is a piece of selenium oxide which generates a tiny electric current when exposed to air.

—4. There are also semiautomatic cameras in which the electric eye is not connected directly to the iris.
—5. The photographer sets the lens opening to correspond with the amount of light registered on the meter.

Exercise B: Name a few kinds of cameras.

www.usps.com

Lesson 28

POST OFFICE

1. Useful Words and Idioms

valuable
postage
to fold
envelope
to register
to check
receipt
to weigh
package
sea mail / air mail
to cost
to deliver
to consist of
to drop
to be impressed at
to amount to
mailman / postman
postal route

2. Common Expressions

P.O. Box
to enclose
mail truck

special / express delivery
telegram
first-class mail
picture card
registered mail
zip code
aerogramme
to put a stamp on the letter
to drop a letter in the mail box
How long does it take for a letter
to get to California?

DIALOGUE

Read the Text:

1. A: What's the postage on this letter to Korea?
   B: Air mail or sea mail?
   A: Air mail please.
   B: That'll be 25 cents.
   A: I'd like to send this package to Korea by sea mail.
   B: Let me check the postage on that.
   A: May I have seven ten-cent stamps and two one-cent stamps?
   B: Okay. That comes to 72 cents in all.

2. A: I'd like to register this letter.
   B: Is there anything valuable in it?
   A: There's a check for one hundred dollars.
   B: Shall I make out a return receipt?
   A: No, don't bother.
   B: That will be seventy-five cents.

Exercise A: Restate your part of the conversation from the text.

1. What's the postage on this letter to Korea?
2. I'd like to send this package to Korea by sea mail.
3. May I have seven ten-cent stamps and two one-cent stamps?
4. Is here anything valuable in it?
5. Shall I make out a return receipt?

Exercise B: Fill in the blanks.

1. He bought some airmail (   ).
3. The clerk wrote the money (   ) for him.
4. Because mail (   ) is such an everyday matter, few people ever stop to think how complicated it is.
5. (   ) mail consists of sealed mail, either letters or parcels and post cards.

COMPOSITION

Read the Text:

Joe wanted to go to the post office yesterday. But he did not want to go alone. He asked me to with him. He was afraid that the people in the post office might no understand his English. He would not go without me. I could not go in the morning, so we went in the afternoon.

First, Joe bought some stamps. He needed five-cent stamps and eighty-cent stamps. He also wanted to mail a package to his family. The package was small. Joe forgot to write his return address on the package. The clerk in the post office told him to put the address on it. Joe could not understand the clerk, so I helped him. Then Joe asked for a money order. He wanted to send some money to his family. The clerk could not understand Joe. I told the clerk what he wanted. The clerk wrote the money order for him. I am glad I with Joe. He needed my help.

Exercise A: Answer the questions 1 to 5 in complete sentences.

1. Where did Joe want to go yesterday?
2. Why didn't he want to go alone?
3. What did he want to mail to his family?
4. What did he forget to write on the package?
5. How did he want to send money to his family?

Exercise B: Make sentences following the example.

Ex: but / want / alone
But he did not want to go alone.

1. he / asked / go with
2. could not / morning / afternoon
3. first / bought / stamps
4. Joe / write / address
5. I / told / what

READING

Read the Text:

Nearly everyone in the world today lives within a few miles of a post office or is reached by a postal delivery service. Because mail service is such an everyday matter, few people ever stop to think how wonderful and complicated it is.

Every year, the United States Post Office handles more than 65 billion pieces of mail in the form of letters newspapers and magazines, and packages. On the average, this amounts to a piece of mail every day for every person in the whole country.

The mail is or has been carried on almost anything that can travel, from donkeyback to jet airplane, from canoes to guided missiles.

In Paris, the post office sends mail within the city through pneumatic tubes. Mail has been dropped by parachute at the South Pole. A mailbag has been dropped from a helicopter into the conning tower of a submarine in the middle of the Pacific Ocean. Mailmen in the Alps daily risk their lives crossing glaciers to reach villages high in the mountains.

Perhaps the greatest thing about the postal service is that it is something in which almost every nation in the world takes part on a willing and equal basis. A letter mailed from New York City to Afghanistan will pass through many countries on its way. Each country will carry it on its postal routes without question. In wartime, mails travel, though often only after censorship and by indirect routes, even between enemy nations.

Exercise A: Indicate whether each of the following statements is true or false by writing the letter T or F in the space provided.

—1. Nearly everyone in the world today lives within a few miles of a post office or is reached by a postal delivery service.
—2. On the average, this amounts to a piece of mail every day for every for every person in the whole country.
—3. The mail is or has carried on anything that can't travel, from donkeyback to jet airplane.
—4. Mailmen in the Alps daily risk their lives crossing glaciers to reach villages high in the mountains.
—5. In wartime, mails can travel, even between enemy nations.

Exercise B: Give a brief account of "First Class" mail.

Lesson 29

MAGAZINE AND NEWSPAPER

1. Useful Words and Idioms

magazine
to issue
weekly / biweekly
monthly / bimonthly
article
headline
journal
to publish
editorial
to forecast
column

to look up
little by little
to get tired of
neither — nor
to be satisfied with
to glance at
a sort of
at a news-stand
on the extreme right

2. Common Expressions

cut
legman
circulation
classified section
reporter / newsman / journalist
advertisement
comics
sports page
editorial
news flash

to cover an event
to be reported n the paper
to deliver the paper
to advertise for work
to publish a paper
to subscribe to a paper
to distribute newspaper

DIALOGUE

Read the Text:

1. A: What magazine do you usually read?
   B: Not any in particular. Sometimes I buy the Reader's Digest. Some of the articles are very interesting and they're very short.
   A: When did you begin to read American magazines and newspapers?
   B: I didn't wait long. It was only a few weeks after I arrived in this country.
   A: Did you understand them?
   B: At the beginning I found them hard, but little by little I began to understand them. They sure helped me a lit with my English.
   A: I guess I'll start reading magazines and newspapers once in a while.
   B: I want to improve my English as soon as possible.

2. A: I've been trying to read this book for the past couple of days, but I find it too difficult every time I try.
   B: Talk about difficult reading! You ought to know what trouble. I have in trying to read English books.
   A: You shouldn't have much trouble. At least not as much as I have because your English is better than my English.
   B: That's not true. I tired of looking up all the new words.

Excercise A: Restate your part of the conversation from the text.

1. What magazine do you usually read?
2. When did you begin to read American magazines?
3. Did you understand them?
4. I've been trying to read this book, but I find it too difficult every time I try.
5. You should have much trouble. At least as much as I have.

Exercise B: Fill in the blanks.

1. A sort of (   ) had its English beginnings with Defoe's Review.
2. (   ) magazines cover special fields such as engineering, chemicals, aviation, etc.
3. (   ) is a periodical usually published weekly or monthly.
4. Many high schools help the pupil read the (   ) newspaper.
5. The child learns to use the school library and the public library to (   ) adventure, sports and mystery for fun.

COMPOSITION

Read the Text:

The American humorist, Will Rogers, used to say, "All I know is what I read in the newspapers." This was an exaggeration for humorous purposes, but it is true that newspapers are an important source of information. Many people begin their day by reading the paper. In this way they learn what is going on in the world. Sometimes, however, they don't have time to read the news carefully and must be satisfied with a quick look at the front page; at other times they may be in such a hurry that they have time only to glance at the headlines.

There are newspapers to satisfy very reader. In the big cities there are many types of papers, with several different editions every day. In small areas the paper is printed weekly.

Most newspapers have several sections, especially on Sundays when the edition is larger than usual. There are, in addition to the front page with the most important news, the sports section, the society page, the comics, the amusement section, a business page and the editorials.

Another type of publication which helps keep the population informed is magazine. Some magazines are published weekly; others are put out monthly. There are news magazines, literary magazines and magazines for such special interests as photography, sports, art and music. Some are primarily for men, others for women and there is a selection of children's magazines, too. In United States, there are publications for every taste and interest.

Exercise A: Answer the questions 1 to 5 in complete sentences.

1. What is the function of a newspaper?
2. Why is a newspaper important?
3. Name three sections of a newspaper.
4. What is the purpose of headlines?
5. Name three types of magazines.

Exercise B: Make sentence following the example.

Ex: all / know / what / newspapers
All I know is what I read in the newspaper.

1. true / newspapers / source
2. people / begin / reading
3. small towns / newspapers / edition
4. publication / informed / magazine
5. publications / taste / interest

READING

Read the Text:

"All I know is what I read in the paper," said Will Rogers, a famous American humorist. Many Americas read the newspaper every day. Some people have it delivered to their homes. Others buy a paper at a news-stand. Every city has a daily newspaper and many cities have several.

The front page (or first page) of the news paper has the most important articles of international. nation and local news. The most important story is in the column on the extreme right. The story second in importance is in the column on the extreme left. Other important news stories take up the rest of page. Appealing "human interest stories" also appear on the front page. Each story has a headline above it. A headline is written in large heavy type. If the news story is very important, the headline may go all the way across the front page. If the story is less important, headline will be only across one column.

Exercise A: Indicate whether each of the following statements true or false by writing the letter T or F in the space provided.

—1. Will Rogers is a famous American inventor.
—2. Some people have it delivered to their homes, others buy a paper at a news-stand.
—3. The most important story is in the column on the extreme front page.
—4. Other important news stories take up the rest of the front page.
—5. If the story is less important, the headline will be only across one column.

Exercise B: Give the names of the Korean newspaper.

BANK

1. Useful Words and Idioms

account
procedure
front desk
check
amount
to cash
to lend
social security card
available
safekeeping

a lot of cash / money
to be kept in the bank
to be modeled after
to fail to
beyond one's ability
in fact
to impose A on B
to be convenient

2. Common Expressions

simple / compound interest
change
bill
loan

remittance
traveller's check
deposit
draft
principal
bankbook / passbook
investment

to open / have / close an account with a bank
to make a loan at a bank
to draw / withdraw money from the bank
the bank
to deposit / put / place money in(at) a bank
to endorse a check
to cash the traveller's check

DIALOGUE

Read the Text:

1. A: Put your name and address here, please.
   B: I want to open an account here.
   A: Where are you employed?
   B: I work for Northwest Orient Airlines.
   A: May I see your driver's license and social security card?
   B: I don't have a social security card, but here's my driver's license and passport.
   A: That's fine.

2. A: Do you cash pay-checks at this bank?
   B: See Mr. Brown owe there at the front desk. He'll tell you.
   A: All right, I'll do that.
   B: Your check was made out in the amount of $ 120.50. That's twenty, forty, sixty eighty, a hundred, a hundred and twenty and fifty cents. $120. 50.

Exercise A: Restate your part of the conversation from the text.

1. Put your name and address here, please.
2. See Mr. Brown over there at the front desk. He will tell you.
3. Do you cash pay checks at this bank?
4. Where are you employed?
5. May I see your driver's license and social security card?

Exercise B: Fill in the blanks.

1. (   ), into which pennies are dropped, often establish the saving habit for the very young.
2. From the borrowers the banks receive (   ) on the sums loaned.
3. Most bank deposits are in the form of (   ) rather than of cash.
4. The housewife sho pa yes her bills by (   ) is fred of the difficulty and danger involved in keeping large sums of cash on hand.
5. The First Bank of the United States, established in 1971, was (   ) after the Bank of England.

COMPOSITION

Read the Text:

A modern bank accepts people's money for safekeeping. It also lends money and offers many other services. The experience of a businessman will show some of these. James Jones has a furniture store and buys his goods from different parts of the country. It isn't convenient for him to send money in his store or in his home. So he goes to the bank and opens a checking account. He puts money in the bank regularly, and the bank keeps it until he writes checks for that amount. When Mr. Jones orders furniture from another city, he simply writes a check. This check is as good as money to the owner of the Modern Furniture Company. He can take it to his bank and cash it, that is, he can get money for it.

Exercise A: Answer the question 1 to 5 in complete sentences.

1. What does a modern bank accept?
2. Where does James Jones buy his good?
3. Is it convenient for him to send money in his store or in his home?
4. What does Mr. Jones write when he orders furniture from another city?
5. Is this check as good as money to the owner of the Modern Furniture Company?

Exercise B: Make sentences following the example.

Ex: modern bank / accept / safekeeping
A modern bank accepts people's money for safekeeping.

1. experience / show / some
2. James Jones / buy / goods
3. He / open / checking account
4. check / good / owner
5. He / take / cash

READING

Read the Text:

The First Bank of the United States, established in 1791, was similarly modeled after the Bank of England. Both the First Bank, which survived until 1811, and the Second Bank, which lasted from 1816, met with strong political opposition. From the closing of the Second Bank until 1836, American banks were chartered only by the states and the laws of the time failed to prevent wild speculation, fraud, bankruptcy, and financial panic. "Wildcat" banks issued patted from hand beyond their ability to redeem; state bank notes passed from hand to hand at varying discounts; and professional money-changers flourished. Counterfeiting was widespread.

Under laws enacted in 1863 and 1864, Congress established the national banking system in order to finance the War between the States by providing a system on which the government could depend and which would inspire public confidence in the currency. The banks were authorized to issue currency on the security of national bonds at 90 per cent of par.

Thus the government at once provided a market for its bonds and a sound basis for paper money. In 1865 Congress drove the state bank notes out of circulation by imposing a 10 per cent tax on them. There were no other fundamental changes in American banking until the establishment of the Federal Reserve System.

Exercise A: Indicate whether each of the following statements in true or false b writing the letter T or F in the space provided.

—1. Both the First Bank and the Second Bank met with strong financial problems.

—2. "Wildcat" banks issued notes a beyond their ability to redeem; state bank notes passed from hand to foot at varying discounts.

—3. The banks were authorized to issue currency on the security of national bonds at 90 per cent of bar.

—4. In 1865 Congress drove the state bank notes out of circulation by imposing a 10 per cent tax on them.

—5. There were no other fundamental changes in American banking until the establishment of the Federal Reserve System.

Exercise B: How many kinds of bank account are there in Korea?

Lesson 31

AMERICAN MONEY

1. Useful Words and Idioms

coin
bill
check
change
cash
value
price
deferred
payment

to cash a check
to be equal to
to be made of
to exchange A for B
to be based on
to be accustomed to
in terms of
in relation to
to act as

2. Common Expressions

American coins: cent
nickel
dime
quarter
half-dollar
dollar

American bills: fiver ($5)
tenner ($10)
century ($100)
grand ($1,000)

DIALOGUE

Read the Text:

1. A: Excuse me, but could I trouble you for some change?
   B: Let me see. Do you want coins?
   A: Can you change this ten-dollar bill?
   B: How do you want it?
   A: A five and five ones, please.
   B: Here you are.
   A: Thank you very much.

2. A: Can I cash a check here?
   B: Do you have an account at this bank?
   A: No, I don't.
   B: Do you have some identification?
   A: Yes, I have passport an this identification card.
   B: That's good enough. What's the amount of the check you want to cash?
   A: It's a government check for $ 129. 37.
   B: O.K.
   A: Thank you.
   B: You're welcome.

Exercise A: Restate your part of the conversation from the text.

1. Excuse me, but could I trouble you for some change?
2. Can you change this ten-dollar bill?
3. Can I cash a check here?
4. Do you have some identification?
5. That's good enough. What's the amount of the check you want to cash.

Exercise B: Fill in the blanks.

1. Metal coins are called (　　).
2. A nickel is worth five (　　).
3. A dime is worth ten (　　).
4. A (　　) is worth twenty-five cents.
5. A fifty cent piece often called a (　　).

COMPOSITION

Read the Text:

American coins are easy to remember. The American dollar is equal to 100 cents or pennies. A half-dollar is 50 cents; a quarter is cents or a fourth of a dollar. A dime is 10 cents; or a tenth of a dollar and a nickel is 5 cents or a twentieth of a dollar. All but the penny and the nickel are made of silver. The penny is made of copper. The nickel is made of a metal called nickel. American silver dollars are not used in many parts of the United States. They are being replaced by paper bills.

In the United States one penny won't buy much, but it is useful to make change. Suppose you had visited the United States ten years ago. For a nickel you might have bought a pencil. For a dime you might have bought an ice cream cone or used a public telephone. A hamburger would have cost you a quarter or more.

Exercise A: Answer the questions 1 to 5 in complete sentences.

1. Is a quarter 25 cent?
2. How much are a quarter and two dimes?
3. What is the penny made of?
4. How many nickels are there in 5 cent?
5. Are silver dollars still used widely in America?

Exercise B: Make sentences following the example.

Ex: American / coins / remember
American coins are easy to remember.

1. dollar / equal / pennies
2. penny / nickel / made of
3. silver / be not used / United States
4. they / replaced / bills
5. dime / bought / ice cream

READING

Read the Text:

We give money to a storekeeper in exchange for some thing we want. This may be a candy bar a model airplane, a pound of cookies, a hat or any one of thousands of articles. We can also exchange money for services such as a haircut and the telephone. Money, we see, is a medium of exchange.

We are so accustomed to thinking of goods in terms of money value that we would have great difficulty if money should pair of shoes. You can buy a good pair for $12 and another ind may cost $18. You know that the $18 shoes probably are better than the $12 ones. Or you are sent to the store to buy a dozen of the best eggs. The grocer tells you the price is sixty cents a dozen. Last month, when eggs were more plentiful, they cost only fifty cents a dozen. These examples show us another of money's purposes or functions: money is often a measure of value. We can also measure and compare the values of articles that are quite unlike by the use of money terms. Suppose we have $10 to spend. With $10 we can buy any of a number of things: a football helmet, a wristwatch, sweater or a few books. Thus, money gives us a convenient way of knowing and comparing the value of things in relation to other things. A third function of money is that ist acts as a standard for deferred payments. This is not quite so easy to understand. Deferred payments are payments to be made at some time in the future.

Exercise A: Indicate whether each of the following statements is true or false by writing the letter T or F in the space provided.

—1. Money, we see, is a medium of exchange.

—2. We are so accustomed to thinking of goods in terms of money value that we would have great convenience if money should suddenly disappear from our lives.

—3. We can also measure and compare the values of articles that are quite unlike by the use of money terms.

—4. Thus, money gives us a convenient way of knowing and

comparing the value of thing in relation to other things.

—5. A third function of money is that it acts as a standard for deferred payments.

Exercise B: Give a brief account of how many kinds of Korean coins there are.

Lesson 32

READING

1. Useful Words and Idioms

classics	to be ashamed
assignment	a lot of
ruler	to be through with
to bother	to make choices
troublesome	to make sure
index cards	to distinguish room
skill	to be unable to
library	to communicate with
effective	to pass on to
environment	to fall in love with

2. Common Expressions

footnote	binding
dime novel	reference
coauthor	copyright
epilogue	paperback
bookworm	piracy
preface	second-hand bookseller
excerpt	to glance over
pulp writer	to read widely
instructive book	to be absorbed in
pornographic	to skip over
who's who	to publish book
royalty	to sit up all night ower a book
	to cry ower a book

DIALOGUE

Read the Text:

1. A: I just finished reading an interesting story.
   B: What was that?
   A: It was *1984* by Orwell.
   B: I'm ashamed to say I haven't done much reading.
   A: I know you've got a lot of things to do.
   B: That's not the only reason.
   A: You really should start reading again.
   B: Could you recommend some thing or me?
   A: This book was well written.

2. A: Are you reading Tess by Thomas Hardy?
   B: Yes, I am.
   A: Are you through with the book?
   B: I'm almost finished with it.
   A: How much more do you have to read?
   B: I only have a few more pages to go.
   A: Tell me something about the story.
   B: It's a very moving story.

Exercise A: Restate your part of the conversation from the text.

1. I just finished reading an interesting story.
2. I know you've got a lot of things to do,
3. Yow really should start reading again.
4. Are you through with the book?
5. How much more do you have to read?

Exercise B: Fill in the blanks.

1. What's the story (　)?
2. Do you (　) for classics?
3. I've read only the (　) versions.
4. The book is a (　) with students.
5. The story was made (　) a movie.

COMPOSITION

Read the Text:

The use of symbols to represent words and ideas is the highest achievement of the superior reasoning power that distinguishes man animals. Reading and writing are man's greatest inventions. Without these skills, man would be unable to share his thoughts with those at a distance in time or place. He would have no historical records. His ability to communicate with fellow man would be much less effective than it is.

There is an old saying that "A dwarf standing on a giant's shoulders sees the farther of the two." This means that man's ability to keep historical records and to read them enables him quickly to acquire the knowledge of the past and to progress to new and greater knowledge. Reading is an adult's most important learned skill and the most important single skill he can pass on to his children. It is the key to all further learning.

Exercise A: Answer the questions 1 to 5 in complete sentences.

1. What is the highest achievement of the superior reasoning power that distinguishes man from animals?
2. What are man's greatest inventions?
3. What enabled man to keep historical records?
4. What is an adult's most important learned skill?
5. What is the key to all further learning?

Exercise B: Make sentences following the example.

Ex: use / is / achievement
The use of symbols to represent words and ideas is the highest achievement of the superior reasoning.

1. reading / writing / inventions
2. without these skills / man / unable
3. ability / communicate / less effective
4. dwarf / sees / farther
5. reading / key / learning

READING

Read the Text:

No author in American literature is better known or more loved than Samuel Lanhorne Clemenns. Born in Missouri in 1835, he grew up on the banks of the Mississippi River and later adopted the pen name of "Mark Twain" from the call of the boatmen on the Mississippi as they measured the depth of the river. The river environment inspired the two novels which brought him his greatest fame: *Tom Sawyer* and *Huckleberry Finn*. Another book, *Life on the Mississippi*, told of his adventures on the river boats of that period.

It was during the Civil War that Mark Twain's life as a writer started. At that time he was working as a newspaper man in Nevada and California. His short story, *The Celebrated Jumping Frog of Calaveras County*, was immediate success and his new career began.

In 1870, Mark Twain married Olivia Langdon. He had fallen in love with her picture even before he met her. According to his biographers, his wife had a great influence on Twain's later books.

Mark Twain was also a very successful lecturer. His travels around the country giving talks on a variety of subjects helped make him famous and increased the sale of his books.

Tom Sawyer and *Huckleberry Finn* are considered Twain's best works. They are marked by humor and satire and provide his readers with an excellent picture of his era. His last boot was completed in 1909, one year before his death. HE was then 74 years old.

Exercise A: Indicate whether each of the following statements is true or false by writing the letter T or F in the space provided.

—1. Mark Twain grew up on the banks of the Mississippi River.
—2. The river environment inspired the two novels which brought him his greatest fame: *Tom Sawyer and Huckleberry Finn*.
—3. It was during the World War that Mark Twain's life as a writer ended.
—4. He had fallen in love with her picture after he had met her.
—5. *Tom Sawyer and Huckleberry Finn* are considered Twain's best works.

Lesson 33

ELECTRONICS

1. Useful Words and Idioms

electronic
automatic
computer
to fix
industry
conductor
employee
to excite
products
device
to be crowed with
to turn up
enough / much money
whether or not
to run out
for the time being
to deal with
by means of
in order to

2. Common Expressions

refrigerator
cutout
mixer
electric fan
washing machine
amplifier
call−phone
vending machine
electronic mattress
electric bulb
stereophonic phonograph
vacuum cleaner
condenser
electric cooker
plug
ventilator
turntable
fluorescent tube

DIALOGUE

Read the Text:

1. A: How do you light this stove?
   B: This is an automatic electronic stove. You can only turn up the wick like this and it lights itself.
   A: Don't you have to pump it up?
   B: You need not.
   A: How often do you have to change the wick?
   B: About six month at normal use.
   A: I'll take one.
   B: Twenty dollars, please.

2. A: Can you give me a hand?
   B: What's wrong?
   A: My computer doesn't work. Could you fix my computer?
   B: Let me see it.
   A: It makes too much noise.
   B: Terminal 10 is down. And power is out.
   A: How long will it take to have it fixed?
   B: It's nothing serious. I can fix it in a few hours.

Exercise A: Restate your part of the conversation from the text.

1. How do you light this stove?
2. Don't you have to pump it up?
3. How often do you have to change the wick?
4. Can you give me a hand?
5. Could you fix my computer?

Exercise B: Fill in the blanks.

1. A computer (   ) orders, and bills customers.
2. Coffee is being (   ) in an electric coffee pot.
3. Bread is being (   ) in an electric toaster.
4. Eggs are (   ) on the electric stove.
5. I (   ) with my electric shaver.

COMPOSITION

Read the Text:

After school, if I have time, I like to ho to the computer game room. The place is usually crowded with other people my age, although, if it's late enough, some older people also come in to play. The games are very exciting and difficult and you'll probably lose if you're playing them for the first time. If I had enough money I would enjoy playing the more difficult games but, unfortunately, I have run out of money, for the time being.

Exercise A: Answer the questions 1 to 5 in complete sentences.

1. What does the author like to do after school?
2. Are young people the only customers?
3. Are the games rather boring and easy?
4. If the author had enough money what would eh do?
5. Does the author have enough money at present?

Exercise B: Make the sentences following the example

Ex: if / time / computer
After school, if I have time, I like to go to the computer game room.

1. place / crowded / my age
2. if / late / older people
3. games / exciting / difficult
4. if / money / difficult
5. unfortunately / run out of / for

READING

Read the Text:

In the United States, many things are sold by machines in bus stations, train stations, airports, public buildings, movies and many other places. Machines sell stamps, newspapers, candy, cigarettes, sandwiches, coffee, chewing gum, soft drinks, cookies; sometimes even stockings and perfume.

Clear directions on how to use the machine are printed on it. You put your money in a slot, usually on the fight-hand side of the machine; then you pull the knob nearest the thing you are buying. Some machines can give change. If you are buying a soft drink for a dime, you can put in a quarter and get your drink and also three nickels in change. Other machines cannot give change; you must have the exact change in order to buy any thing. The instructions on the machine will tell you whether or not you must use the exact change.

An employee of the vending machine company comes every day or every week, depending on the kind of product sold in the machine, to fill it and to take out money.

Exercise A: Indicate whether each of the following statements is true or false by writing the letter T or F in the space provided.

—1. In the United States, many things are sold by men in many places.
—2. You put your money in a slot; then you pull the knob nearest the thing you are buying.
—3. If you are buying a soft drink for a dime, you can put in a quarter and get your drink and also three nickels in change.
—4. You must have the exact change in order to buy any thing.
—5. The instructions on the machine will tel you whether or not you must use the exact change.

Exercise B: How many kinds of electric tools are there in Korea?

Lesson 34

CAMPUS LIFE

1. Useful Words and Idioms

midterm exams
dormitory
library
athletic filed
stadium
thermostat
lodge
instructor / professor
lecture
to assign
to get worried
to get a good view of
language laboratory
to stroll about
on the tenth floor
on the whole
to go off campus
a lot of
in the wintertime
to jump over

2. Common Expressions

term paper
thesis
quiz
flunk
pass
credit
cut
undergraduate student
graduate student
freshman
sophomore
junior
senior
tuition
quarter
curriculum
faculty
major
minor
final
cram
house mother
fraternity
co-educational

DIALOGUE

Read the Text:

1. A: Do enjoy your college life?
   B: I feel each day at college passes very quickly.
   A: I never thought I'd be so busy.
   B: Besides our regular classes, we've got many extracurricular activities.
   A: They demand a lot of time.
   B: They demand a lot of time.
   B: Most of us are engaged in part-time jobs.
   A: In your case, too?
   B: Of course, I don't have a minute to spare.

2. A: When are midterm exams?
   B: Midterms will be given at the end of April.
   A: I'm really beginning to get worried about them.
   B: Don't worry. You'll do fine.
   A: What will the history midterm be like?
   B: It'll be easy exam.

Exercise A: Restate your part of the conversation from the text.

1. Do you enjoy your college life?
2. In your case, too?
3. When are midterm exams?
4. I'm really beginning to get worried about them.
5. What will the history midterm be like?

Exercise B: Fill in the blanks.

1. (   ) is a long paper, usually anywhere from three thousand to five thousand words in length about a special subject.
2. (   ) is anyone who has not yet received his bachelor's degree.
3. (   ) is money paid to the school for the cost of schooling.
4. (   ) is a building where students live.
5. (   ) is the woman who is in charge of a dormitory.

COMPOSITION

Read the Text:

My parents visited me at college last week. Before their train arrived at the station, it passed by the campus located on the college from the distance. I am proud of the college buildings and grounds and I wanted to show my parents everything. First, we walked around the campus and looked at the buildings from the outside and then I took them through the dormitory, the library, the language laboratory and the science building. We went up and down the halls of the science building, looking into the classrooms. After that, we went across the athletic field and into the stadium. My father, who had played soccer in college, jumped over a low hedge between the seats and the playing field. He said that merely seeing the field made him feel like a young man again. Leaving the stadium, we visited the university museum of modern art and went off campus to have dinner. After dinner, we strolled about the quiet campus until bedtime.

Exercise A: Answer the questions 1 to 5 in complete sentences.

1. When did the author's parents visit him?
2. Was it possible to get a good view of the campus before arriving?
3. How did the author's father react when he saw the athletic field?
4. Did they have dinner on campus?
5. What did they do after dinner?

Exercise B: Make sentences following the example.

Ex: proud / buildings / grounds
I am proud of the college buildings and grounds.

1. wanted / show / everything
2. walked around / looked / outside
3. took / laboratory / science
4. went / athletic / stadium
5. said / seeing / feel like

READING

Read the Text:

Professors and instructors in American schools are usually very friendly with students. Most classes are informal. The teachers almost always welcome discussion. You will be surprised and students. Most professors are available in their offices during certain hours of the day or by appointment to discuss any special problems with the students.

There are, of course, many methods of teaching used in college classes—lectures, discussions, etc. The student may ask the instructor questions during the class period and the instructor will probably ask the students questions. The teacher will often assign written reports and maybe even some oral report. You may have several tests during the course and a final examination at the end of the semester. For each class period, the student is expected to spend at least two hours outside the class period in preparation. Most colleges have a certain policy regarding the amount of times you may miss any class during a semester—usually about three unexcused "cuts." An absence is generally excused for sickness or death in the family. A thorough knowledge of English is necessary in order to study in America. You will only be wasting your time if you go unprepared. If you cannot readily understand the English in this book, you are not yet ready to go.

Exercise A: Indicate whether each of the following statements is true or false by writing the letter T or F in the space provided.

—1. The teachers often welcome discussion.

—2. The teachers will often assign written reports and may be even some oral reports.

—3. For each class period, the teachers are expected to spend at least two hours outside the class period in preparation.

—4. An absence is generally excused for fishing or picnic in the family.

—5. If you cannot readily understand the English in this book, you are not yet ready to go.

Exercise B: Give a brief account of your campus life.

LIBRARY

1. Useful Words and Idioms

card catalog
classification
to borrow
open shelf / stack library
loan desk
librarian
public / school library
library week
to foster
radio / television station
collection
to pay a fine
to set aside
to be looking for
in turn
in addition to
to be likely to
in short
in fact
to focus attention on
to serve as

2. Common Expressions

borrower
to be shelved
to select
reference books
periodica
current magazines
microprint
microfilm
book number
classification number
title card
subject card
Dewey classification number

DIALOGUE

Read the Text:

1. A: Where can I find this book?
   B: The card catalog will tell you its location.
   A: How long can I keep the book?
   B: You may keep the book for one week.
   A: What happens if I return the book late?
   B: You should pay a fine in that case.

2. A: Here we are at the library. I want to get a good story to read.
   B: Are they many different departments in the library?
   A: Yes, there are several departments.
   Here is the fiction department where I'll get my story.
   B: Can you borrow all these books?
   A: Most of the books here can be borrowed.
   B: There are a lot of people reading in that room.
   What kinds of boos are in there?
   A: Those are the magazines and newspapers.

Exercise A: Restate your part of the conversation from the text.

1. Where can I find this book?
2. How long can I keep the book?
3. What happens if I return the book late?
4. Here we are at the library. I want to get a good story to read.
5. Can you borrow all these cooks?

Exercise B: Fill in the blanks.

1. The S.O.S.U. Library is an "open (   )" library.
2. Borrowers are expected to acquaint (   ) with this system.
3. When consulting the card catalog for a desired book, (   ).
4. to the floor and section where that classification of book is shelved, (   ) the book.
5. and (   ) it out at the main loan desk.

COMPOSITION

Read the Text:

The library provides many services to people, but its chief value lies in providing access to the huge volume of printed mater that exists in the modern world.

Every citizen and certainly every student should learn how to use the library properly. If there is a book you are looking for, you can find it if you know its exact title, the author's name, or even its general subject matter. Sometimes the librarian can be helpful in locating some hard-to-find work. In addition to its collection of books, most libraries also have a periodical section which houses the library's collection of newspapers, magazines and journals; in short, information of topical interest.

Libraries are extremely popular in Korea. They are so popular, in fact, that most public and school libraries are rowed from early morning until closing time, and an empty eat is difficult to find.

Exercise A: Answer the questions 1 to 5 in complete sentences.

1. What is the chief value of a library?
2. How can you find a book in the library?
3. Of what is the periodical section comprised?
4. Why do students like to study there?
5. Is it easy to find a seat in the library?

Exercise B: Make sentences following the example.

Ex: library / provides / services
The library provides many services to example.

1. chief value / access / huge volume
2. citizen / certainly / properly
3. libraries / popular / Korea
4. sometimes / locating / hard-to-find
5. empty / difficult / find

READING

Read the Text:

LIBRARY. The name library comes from the Latin word librarius, which in turn comes from liber, meaning a book. In the literal sense, therefore, a library is a collection of books. As time passed, the word library also came to mean a place — a room or a building — in which books are kept. Today, when speak of the library, we think not only of the books and the place where they are kept, but also of the services provided by the librarians and their assistants. These services are intended to make the books as useful as possible to the users of the library.

Libraries began in societies in which the ability to read and write was limited to a small part of the population, as in Babylonia and ancient Egypt. These first libraries were organized to store the official records of the government and the religious writing of the priests. Today we take books and other forms of reading matter for granted and use them constantly. We are likely to forget how valuable books were in the past, when they were very scarce, and how important they were in preserving the essential elements of early cultures and in transmitting them from generation to generation

Originally, then, the library (and the materials it contained) was an institution created to preserve the accumulated knowledge of one generation so that it could be passed on to the next — it served as the memory of its society.

Exercise A: Indicate whether each of the following statements is true or false by writing the letter T or F in the space provided.

1. The name library comes from the Latin word librarius, which in turn comes from liber, meaning a book.
2. As time passed, the word library didn't come to mean a place —a room or a building — in which books are kept.
3. Today we take books and other forms of reading matter for granted and use them constantly.

4. We aren't likely to forget how valuable books were in the past, when they were very scarce.
5. Originally, then, the library (and the materials it contained) was an institution created to preserve the accumulated knowledge of one generation so that it could be passed on to the next.

Exercise B: Give a brief account of your college library.

PIZZA
BURGERS
FISH CHIPS
RADIO TAIRUA

DAILY LIFE

1. Useful Words and idioms

breakfast / lunch / dinner
homework / assignment
secretary
to brush
bus stop
to take off
to put on
pants / socks
to wait for
to work in
to be born in
first / given name
to get up
to take a shower
to get dressed
as soon as
next to
to go to bed / get into bed
to fall asleep
to refresh oneself
to take a break
once n a while
to talk on the telephone

2. Common Expressions

1. Morning

A. At what time do you get up in the morning?
B. What do you do before you leave for school or work?

2. Getting to School or Work and the Afternoon

A. How do you get to school or work?
B. What are your hours at school or work?
C. What do you do afterwards?

3. Evening

A. What do you do when you get home?
B. What do you do after dinner?
C. How do you prepare for bed?

DIALOGUE

Read the Text:

1. A: Do you get up early in the morning?
   B: Yes. I get out of bed about 6:30 every morning.
   A: After getting up, you take a shower, don't you?
   B: Yes, I do. Then I brush my teeth and get dressed.
   A: What time do you gave breakfast?
   B: At seven. I have a light one.
   A: What do you have for breakfast.
2. A: As soon as you get home from school, what do you do?
   B: I sit down and do my homework.
   A: What time do you eat dinner?
   B: At seven o'clock I eat dinner with my brother.
   A: Well, do you go to bed soon?
   B: No, I watch television for an hour or two, read, or write leers. At about ten, I get into bed, and fall asleep.

Exercise A: Restate your part of the conversation from the Text.

1. Do you get up early in the morning?
2. After getting up, you take a shower, don't you?
3. What time do you have breakfast?
4. What do you do after dinner?
5. What time do you go to bed?

Exercise B: Fill in the blanks.

1. How (   ) days you work in a weeks?
2. What time are young going to (   ) lunch?
3. How was your (   )?
4. What do you have (   ) dinner?
5. I refreshed (   ) with a cup of coffee?

COMPOSITION

Read the Text:

It is seven thirty in the morning. Mr. Green gets out of bed. He goes into the bathroom and washes. He dries his hands and face on the towel and then brushes his teeth. Then he dresses.

He puts o his shirt and pants, shoes and socks, and his tie. Then he puts on his get and jacket. Mr. Green is a mailman, he wears a uniform. At a quarter past eight he kisses his wife and children good-bye. He is late this morning. The bus comes at twenty past eight. Mr. Green hurries to the bus stop. He sees the bus. He runs and tries to catch the bus, but he misses it. He waits for the nest bus. He is late for work. It is raining and there is a puddle next to the bus stop. When the bus comes, it splashes Mr. Green. Mr. Green carries the bag on his back. It is very heavy today because there is a lot of mail. At four o'clock he opens the gate of the last house. He is very tired. A dog comes out of the house and chases Mr. Green. The dog bites a hole in his pants. "Oh," cries Mr. Green, "What a day."

Exercise A: Answer the questions 1 to 5 in complete sentences.

1. What does Mr. Green do at seven thirty?
2. What does he put on?
3. What does he do at a quarter past eight?
4. What does the bus do?
5. What does he do at four?

Exercise B: Make sentences following the example.

Ex: goes into / bathroom / washes
He goes into the bathroom and washes.

1. dries / towel / brushes
2. Mr. Green / mailman / uniform
3. runs / tries / misses
4. raining / puddle / stop
5. heavy / lot / mail

READING

Read the Text:

My name is Frank Ryan and I am a teacher of languages. I was born in 1940 in a little country town not far from here. I have a brother who is three years older than I am, and a sister who is two years younger than I am. My brother's first name is Henry and my sister's name is Nancy. There are five of us in my family. My father and mother get up early every morning. My mother gets up at about 6 a.m. and my father gets up at about at 6:30. I don't get up until 7 o'clock or 8 o'clock. My brother gets up earlier than I do, and I get up earlier than my sister does. Some days I get up at 7: 30 and some days I don't get up until almost 8 o'clock.

After I wake up each morning, I get up and get dressed. After I get dressed, I have breakfast. Usually, I have a light breakfast but my brother has a big breakfast. I have juice, cereal and coffee for breakfast. Once in a while I have buttered toast too. My brother, Henry, usually has juice, oatmeal, toast and two or three cups of coffee. My sister, Nancy, just has juice and toast for breakfast. We finish eating breakfast at about 8:15 or 8:30 every morning. I usually leave the house at 8:50 each morning and work hard all morning and go out for lunch at about 12:30. My brother leaves the house earlier than I do, and he gets to work at 8:45 each morning.

I finish working at about 5:45 p.m. My sister finishes working earlier than I do, and my brother finishes working later than I do. We usually have dinner at about 7:15 and after dinner we read the newspaper for a while or listen to the radio. Once in a while my sister talks on the telephone and my brother watches television. We usually go to bed at about midnight.

Exercise A: Indicate whether each of the following statements is true or false by writhing the letter T or F in the space provided.

—1. Frank Ryan was born in 1940 in a little country town not far from here.

—2. Henry and Nancy get up early every morning.
—3. My sister, Nancy, just has juice and toast for breakfast.
—4. My brother gets to work at 9 o'clock each morning.
—5. We usually go to bed at about 8:15 or 8:30.

Exercise B: What is your favorite program on KBS-1 TV?

Lesson 37

EDUCATION

1. Useful Words and Idioms

summer / winter school
to solve
regular class
public / private
scholarship
compulsory
superintendent
fund
curriculum

not only A also B
to be about
on the basis of
to come from
in the hands of
to vary from A to B
to consist of
according to
to pay for
to be responsible for
in addition

2. Common Expressions

liberal arts college
university
junior college
business college
teachers college
Professional school
adult education
public school
private school
church school

the system of evaluating
student's work
A(excellent) 100–93%
B(good: above average) 92–86%
C(average) 85–80%
D(below average) 79–75%
F(failing) 74 or below

graduate degrees:
B.A. Bachelor of Arts
M.A. Master of Arts
M.S. Master of Science
M.D. Doctor of Medicine
Ph.D. Doctor of Philosophy
L.D. Doctor of Law

DIALOGUE

Read the Text:

1. A: You speak English so well. Where did you learn it?
   B: At our college. In addition to regular classes, we had English summer school every year.
   A: There you were required to speak only English, I suppose?
   B: Yes, not only in class but also at meals an during recreation. We worked very hard.
   A: How long did summer school last?
   B: Ten days. We wished we had more, but we tried to make the best of the short session.

2. A: What is the trouble with our education today?
   B: I think they drill too much on business and technology.
   A: Do you have any solutions?
   B: Yes, I have. I'm sure it's developing one's character.
   A: What is developing one's character?
   B: It is to find the real, unlimited being.
   A: How can we get it?
   B: It can be developed by good study under inspired teachers.

Exercise A: Restate your part of the conversation from the text.

1. You speak English so well. Where did you learn it?
2. How long did summer school last?
3. What is the trouble with our education today?
4. Do you have any way to solve it?
5. What is developing one's character?

Exercise B: Fill in the blanks.

1. In the United States, a child usually begins his formal education when he is about ( ) years old.
2. Children frequently go to nursery school or ( ) before entering first grade.
3. In larger cities there are ( ) classes and Saturday class for adults.
4. American colleges are usually run on a ( ) basis.
5. Many college students earn part or all of their ( ) by working their way through college.

COMPOSITION

Read the Text:

Education is compulsory and free for every child in the United States. Most children start school by the age of six. They attend eight years of elementary school and four years of high school(or secondary school). The money for free public schools comes from taxes, and each state is responsible for its own educational system. State legislatures set the educational requirements but leave the management of the schools in the hands of the local communities. Most states require their children to go to school until a certain age. This age varies from 16 to 18 years according to the laws of the individual states. The Federal government contributes funds to the states for an additional schools and school services.

Exercise A: Answer the questions 1 to 5 in complete sentences.

1. At what age do most children start school?
2. How many years do they attend elementary school?
3. How many years do they attend high school?
4. Where does the money for public schools come from?
5. Who is responsible for the educational system?

Exercise B: Make sentences following the example.

Ex: education / compulsory / free / U. S.
Education is compulsory and free for every child in the U.S.

1. children / school / age
2. money / public / taxes
3. legislatures / leave / management
4. states / require / children
5. varies / according / laws

READING

Read the Text:

American schools, both public and private, consist of 12 years of grades–basically 8 years of elementary school and 4 years of secondary or high school, although grades 7 and 8, 7, 8 and 9 may be housed together in middle school or junior high school. In addition, the elementary school offers five–year–olds a year of kindergarten, usually half–day sessions, before they have formal instruction in reading and writing in the first grade. In a few states two year of junior college (the first two years of higher education) or a vocational school are part of the public school system. Schooling is compulsory in most states to the age of 16.

The public schools are administered by local school boards–groups of people elected by the voters. The board appoints the superintendent and sometimes participates in choosing the teachers, in establishing the curriculum. In 1975–1976 local government provided about 47 percent of the revenue per pupil, and the states contribute about 44 percent. Local funds for the schools come largely from property taxes paid by residents of the local school districts. Thus the people of the entire community, not just th e parents of the children who attend, pay for the public schools, which are free and open to everyone.

Exercise A: Indicate whether each of the following statements is true or false by writing the letter T or F in the space provided.

1. American schools consist of 16 years of grades.
2. Schooling is compulsory in most states to the age of 16.
3. The public schools are administered by local school boards–groups of people elected by the voters.
4. In 1975–1976 local government provided about 44 percent of the revenue per pupil
5. Local funds for the schools come largely from property taxes paid by residents of the local school districts.

Exercise B: How does a student support himself during his college years?

Lesson 38

TRAFFIC

1. Useful Words and Idioms

map
stranger
block
street / avenue
the police
accident
insurance
pedestrian
to spur
license

to get to
to be heavy
to go across
to get lost

to be killed in
to be knocked over by
to be dressed in
to amount to
along with

2. Common Expressions

boulevard
block-number
signboard
skyscraper
junction
traffic lights
signal
landmark
to drop
parking lot
traffic accident
hit and run

to stop on red
to take a short cut
to be jammed
to watch out for
Drive
Detour
Dead end
Proceed with caution

DIALOGUE

Read the Text:

1. A: I'm afraid we don't have a map.
   B: That's O.K. We can't lose our way.
   A: But we're strangers here.
   B: The names of the streets are numbers.
   A: We want to go to 42nd Street.
   B: We're on 39th Street. So we go three blocks north.
   A: Where's north?
   B: Look at the numbers on the buildings. The low numbers are south and the high numbers north.

2. A: Excuse me. Can you tell me how to get to the post office?
   B: Of course. It's very near here. Go to the corner and turn right. Walk one block and turn right again. Go across the street. The post office is on the corner. You can't miss it.
   A: Thank you very much. I'm sure I'll find it.
   B: There's one thing. I forgot to tell you.
   A: What's that?
   B: Today is a holiday. The post office is closed.

Exercise A: Restate your part of the conversation from the text.

1. I'm afraid we don't have a map.
2. We want to go to 42nd Street.
3. What's north?
4. Excuse me. Can you tel me how to get to the post office?
5. What's that?

Exercise B: Fill in the blanks.

1. ( ) direction is it to the university?
2. How did you ( ) lost?
3. ( ) is the shortest way?
4. ( ) far is it to the church?
5. The traffic's very ( ).

COMPOSITION

Read the Text:

The problem of accident prevention is an ever-present one on all streets and highways. It is a human as well as an economic problem. Nearly 40,000 persons are killed in street and highway accidents every year. About 1,500,000 are injured in such accidents yearly, many of them permanently crippled. Traffic accidents cost the American people four and a half property damage, and the estimated potential earnings of those killed or disabled. About tone out of five persons killed in traffic is a pedestrian. Pedestrian traffic deaths are most numerous in cities, and in some cities amount to 75 per cent of the traffic victims.

Exercise A: Answer the questions 1 to 5 in complete sentences.

1. What is a human as well as an economic problem?
2. How many persons are killed in street and highway accidents every year?
3. How many persons are injured in such accidents yearly?
4. How many dollars do traffic accidents cost the American people a year?
5. Who is about one out of five persons killed in traffic?

Exercise B: Make the sentences following the example.

Ex: human / as well as / economic problem
It is a human as well as an economic problem.

1. problem / prevention / ever-present
2. nearly / killed / accidents
3. many / injured / crippled
4. traffic / cost / the American people
5. one / killed / pedestrian

READING

Read the Text:

Along with the Federal road–building program came efforts to prevent accidents. By the early 1920's highway accidents were killing and injuring thousands of people every year.

The first national high–safety conference was called in 1924 by Herbert Hoover, then Secretary of Commerce. Thereafter such conferences were held yearly or oftener. In 946 the continuing interest of the Executive branch of the government took the form of the Presidents Conference, later called the White House Conference, on Highway Safety. The President's Committee for Traffic Safety continues to be the agency that draws together and spurs the efforts of state and city officials, safety groups, business, and industry to work for better, safer use of highway.

In the United States, motor vehicles travel about 750,000,000,000 miles a year, or a average of 4, 160 miles per person. There are about 90,000,000 licensed motor–vehicle operators in the nation, including passenger–car drivers, and chauffeurs or commercial vehicle operators. All states require drivers to have licenses. Rules governing legal driving age and length of license validity vary in individual states.

Exercise A: Indicate whether each of the following statements is true or false by writing the letter T or F in the space provided.

—1. By the early 1920's highway accident were killing and injuring thousands of people every year.
—2. Thereafter such conferences were held yearly or oftener.
—3. In 1924 the continuing interest of the Executive branch of the government took the form of the President's Conference.
—4. All states require drivers to have licenses.
—5. Rules governing legal driving age and length of license validity vary in individual state.

Exercise B: How many licensed motor–vehicle operators are there in Seoul?

Lesson 39

MEDICAL

1. Useful Words and Idioms

checkup
trouble
pulse
temperature
injection
intern
medicine
drug-store
illness
patient
contagious

to be sick / injured
to be examined by
to be over
to be healthy
to be divided into
to be limited to
in the field of
to be taken from
to be similar to

2. Common Expressions

disease: anemia
appendicitis
athlete's foot
diabetes
encephalitis
gallstone
hypertension
leukemia
rheumatism
chicken pox
measles
typhoid
cataract
bronchitis
influenza / flu
cold
consumption
neuralgia

DIALOGUE

Read the Text:

1. A: Dr. Park's office.
   B: This is George Jones speaking.
   Can I come sometime this week?
   A: Is something wrong?
   B: Just my regular six months' checkup.
   A: Let's make it nest week, then.
   B: That will be fine.

2. A: Now, what's your trouble, young friend?
   B: I don't feel well. I feel hot and have a headache.
   A: Have you taken your temperature?
   B: Yes, it was normal this morning.
   A: Let me feel your pulse. Well, that's normal, too.
   Open your mouth. Let's see. . . . your throat is very red.
   B: Yes, I forgot to tell your that.

Exercise A: Restate your part of the conversation from the text.

1. Dr. Park's office.
2. Is something wrong?
3. Now, what's your trouble, young friend.
4. Have you taken your temperature?
5. Let me feel your pulse. Well, that's normal, too.
   Your throat is very red.

Exercise B: Fill in the blanks.

1. I think it's just a bad cold. I'll give you an (   ).
2. An injection is better than (   ) in your case.
3. Voluntary hospitals are (   ) and are usually physicians, assisted by resident physicians and interns.
4. Medical service is under the direction of (   ) physicians, assisted by resident physicians and interns.
5. (   ) is a building in which the sick or injured receive care.

COMPOSITION

Read the Text:

There is this story about Daniel Webster, who was famous American of the nineteenth century. Once, Daniel Webster went into a drug-store in order to buy some medicine.

"I want something for a headache," he said to the druggist.

A bottle of ammonia happened to be standing on the counter, so the druggist pocked it up and held it under Webster's nose. The smell, however, was very strong and Webster became quite sick. He almost fainted. He also became very angry with the druggist.

"But didn't it help your headache?" asked the druggist.

"My headache?" said Webster. "I haven't any headache. It's my wife who has the headache."

Exercise A: Answer the questions 1 to 5 in complete sentences.

1. Who was Daniel Webster?
2. What was standing on the counter?
3. What happened to Webster after he smelled the ammonia?
4. Was he pleased or angry with the druggist?
5. Who was it that had a headache?

Exercise B: Make sentences following the example.

Ex: there / story / Daniel Webster
There is this story about Daniel Webster.

1. drug-store / order / medicine
2. want / for / headache
3. druggist / picked / nose
4. became / angry / druggist
5. my wife / who / headache

READING

Read the Text:

HOSPITAL, a building or group of buildings in which the sick or injured receive care. There are thousands of hospitals in the world for plants, birds, animals and humans. The hospitals in which people are treated can be divided into two large groups. The general hospital is one that accepts all types of patients; the special hospital is limited to patients with certain types of illnesses. Most hospitals are general. They admit about nine tenths of all patients. Special hospitals, however, give very important services in the fields of mental care, maternity care and contagious diseases.

The word hospital is taken from the Latin word hospitium, meaning house for guests. The first hospitals, many years before the time of Christ, were similar to the hostels of today. Most of the sick or infirmwere cared for at home unless they were alone or too poor for private attention. European communities began to build hospitals in the early 1700's but these were operated as charity institutions and to isolate victims of contagious disease. Only as the medical and nursing professions developed and new techniques such as anesthesia were discovered did the hospital gradually grow into its efficient modern form. The first hospitals in America were established in Mexico City and in what is today part of New York City.

Exercise A: Indicate whether each of the following statements is true or false by writing the leer T or F in the space provided.

—1. The hospitals in which people are treated can be divided into two large groups.
—2. The general hospital is limited to patients with certain types of illnesses.
—3. The special hospitals admit about nine-tenths of all doctors.
—4. The first hospitals were not similar to the hostels of today.
—5. European communities began to build hospitals in the early 1700's.

Exercise B: If you have your tooth problem, what would you do at first?

RELIGION

1. Useful Words and Idioms

sin
atheist
heaven
sacrament
salvation
protestant
monotheism
to exert
followers
faith
eternal life
the Perfect Being
to be provided
to be worshiped
to be concerned with
apart from
to be committed
to escape from

2. Common Expressions

Christianity
Islam
Hinduism
Confucianism
Buddhism
Shintoism
Taoism
Judaism
paradise / heaven
priest / pastor / minister
atheism
pagoda
monastery / temple
sermon
hym / sacred song
choir
pulpit / altar
shrine
psalms
believer / the faithful
crucifix
to tell one's beads
to attend service
Lord's Prayer

DIALOGUE

Read the Text:

1. A: How can I wash away my sin?
   B: Why don't you go to church? That's the only way.
   A: But I can't see God with my eyes and reason.
   B: You can only meet God with love and freedom.
   A: I don't understand just what sin means.
   B: That's a trial and error on the way to the Perfect Idea. Jesus guides us into heaven.
   A: Where is heaven?
   B: Where there is the Perfect Being, there's heaven.
   A: Isn't it a place?
   B: No, it isn't.

2. A: Why don't you have a religion?
   B: I am an atheist.
   A: How do you live in this suffering world?
   B: I think life is a destiny route.
   A: God is love. Love is Great Creator, not a fatal creature.
   B: What means love?
   A: Love bears all things.
   B: But after this world, I'm sure I'll gain nothing.
   A: Love guides you to the eternal life. Have a religion.

Exercise A: Restate your part of the conversation from the text.

1. How can I wash away my sin?
2. But I can't see God with my eyes and reason.
3. I don't understand just what sin means.
4. Why don't you have a religion?
5. What means love?

Exercise B: Fill in the blanks.

1. Religion is a way of life arising from a (   ) in a Supreme Being or Beings.
2. In the religions of primitive cultures, natural objects or

the spirits of ancestors have been ( ).

3. Such religions as Judaism, Buddhism have had men called ( ).
4. Church may refer to the whole community of ( ) believers.
5. Major faiths of Asia are Hinduism, Shintoism, Taoism, Buddhism and ( ).

COMPOSITION

Read the Text:

The three great monotheistic religions are Christianity, Islam and Judaism. The majority of Christians lives in Europe and North and South America; of Moslems, in Asia and Africa; and of Jews, in North America, Europe, and Asia (primarily Israel). These religions have exerted great influence on history. Another monotheism, Zoroastrianism, also historically important, now has only a small group of followers, all in Asia.

Major faiths of Asia are Hinduism, Confucianism, Buddhism, Shintoism and Taoism. Among the rest of the world's peoples, a great variety of minor cults and faiths exist. Approximate percentages of the world's religious population for each of the major groups are given in the following table:

Religion	Percentage
Christianity	30.7
Islam	14.7
Hinduism	11.4
Confucianism	11.2
Buddhism	5.2
Shintoism	2.0
Taoism	1.7
Judaism	0.4
Others	22.7

Exercise A: Answer the questions 1 to 5 in the complete sentences.

1. What are the three great monotheistic religions?
2. Where does the majority of Christians live?
3. Where does the majority of Moslems live?
4. What are major faiths of Asia?

Exercise B: Make sentences following the example.

Ex: three / monotheistic / are / Christianity / Islam / Judaism
The three great monotheistic religions are Christianity, Islam and Judaism.

1. majority / lives / America
2. religions / exerted / history
3. Zoroastrianism / followers / Asia
4. major / faiths / Asia
5. rest / cults / faiths

READING

Read the Text:

Religions may be classified as polytheism, in which many gods are worshiped, or monotheisms, in which only one supreme being is worshiped.

Religion has taken many forms. In the religions of savages or of primitive cultures, natural objects or the spirits of ancestors have been worshiped. Among such primitive peoples, fear is often the primary stimulus to religious observance. Magical rites and ceremonies are an important part of this observance, where the priests is an intermediary between man and the objects of worship. In the religions of more advanced cultures, such as those of ancient Egypt, Greece, and Rome, magic gave way to mythology, and priests began to show some concern with morals. In the religions of higher civilizations, the spiritual nature of man and the importance of his relation to the divine are emphasized. Love, charity, humility, devotion, and other virtues are required of the followers of such religions. Some of the religions of the Far East place such emphasis on the wretchedness of human existence and the desirability of escape from life that an attitude of passivity and resignation is developed become mere ethical systems. Between these extremes are the religions which demand high ethical standards; without losing sight of the spiritual nature of man.

Exercise A: Indicate whether each of the following statements is true or false by writing the letter T or F in the space provided.

—1. Worshipping many gods is Monotheism.
—2. In the religions of civilized cultures, natural objects or the spirits of ancestors have been worshiped.
—3. Among such primitive peoples, fear is often the primary stimulus to religious observance.
—4. Love, charity, humility, devotion and other virtues are required of the followers of religions of higher civilizations.
—5. Other faiths disregard the spiritual to such an extent that they become mere ethical systems.

Exercise B: Do you have a religion? Why?

Lesson 41

COURT

1. Useful Words and Idioms

debtor	to appeal to the law
lawyer	to be on the rocks
innocence	to end up
sentence	to fall apart
the accused	to be alike
jurisdiction	more or less
pension	to hold of
attorney	to be passed by
marshal	to settle disputes

2. Common Expressions

private means	to imprison
appeal	to keep the law
notary	to break / violate the law
dismissal	to face a trial
convict	to be involved in
lawyer	to be spurred
crime	to perjure / give false evidence
witness	
innocent	

DIALOGUE

Read the Text:

1. A: How can I be paid back from my debtor?
   B: Do you have securities?
   A: No, I've had the bill fallen due?
   B: Was it notarized?
   A: Yes, by my lawyer.
   B: Let's appeal to the law.

2. A: Is your marriage on the rocks?
   B: We have irreconcilable differences.
   A: Look on the bright side.
   B: That doesn't help anything.
   A: Remember back when you were so much in love.
   B: I don't feel the same way now.
   A: Your way of thinking will make you end up in court.
   B: Our marriage has fallen apart.

Exercise A: Restate your part of the conversation from the text.

1. How can I paid back from my debtor?
2. Was it notarized?
3. Is your marriage on the rocks?
4. Look on the bright side.
5. Remember back when you were so much in love.

Exercise B; Fill in the blanks.

1. The lawyer pleaded (　) his innocence.
2. I'll sue you (　) abusing my human rights.
3. He will be tried (　) spying for the enemy.
4. He was (　) a hard labor for 10 years.
5. The judge (　) the murder charge against him.

COMPOSITION

Read the Text:

COURT, a tribunal established for the administration of justice. Courts existed among the earliest primitive tribes and were even elaborately organized in ancient Greece and Rome. The court systems of modern nations differ widely, but the composition, purpose and general powers of all are more or less alike. However, those of the English-speaking countries are especially noted for their protection of the rights of the accused and of the individual against governmental tyranny and oppression.

Excepting the Supreme Court, most of the Federal courts of the United States are concerned principally with cases and controversies involving the administration of Federal laws. Such cases start in the proper District Court and usually are finally disposed of there; if not, they may be carried to a Circuit Court of Appeals, and under certain conditions may reach the Supreme Court. In addition to theses three courts, there are several having jurisdiction over certain special matters.

Exercise A: Answer the questions 1 to 5 in complete sentences.

1. Why is a tribunal established?
2. Did courts exist among the earliest primitive tribes?
3. What are more or less alike in the court systems of modern nations?
4. What are those of the English-speaking countries noted for?
5. What are most of the Federal courts of the United States concerned principally with?

Exercise B: Make the sentences following the example.

Ex: tribunal / established / administration / justice
A tribunal established for the administration of justice.

1. courts / existed / tribes
2. systems / nations / differ
3. general / are / alike
4. Federal / concerned / cases
5. several / jurisdiction / matters

READING

Read the Text:

Courts have been developed to interpret and to apply th law and to settle disputes arising between individuals and groups. Although methods of hearing and deciding cases vary, the purpose of all courts is to determine the facts involved, to insure the administration of justice, and to protect the rights of all. Each court has one or more judges to see that its proceedings are carried out according to the law and to decide what evidence may be admitted. As officers of the court, attorneys also are expected to assist in determining the facts and in seeing that the laws are fairly administered.

Trial by an impartial jury of one's peers has also long been regarded as a right and a guarantee of justice, and has become an established part of the legal system of many countries.

Many courts have clerks to keep their records and such other duties as keeping order in court and having charge of prisoners in the courtroom and of juries during trial (so that they may not be influenced by outside pressures). Although court calendars are often so clogged with pending cases that trials are delayed, which keeps persons from being arrested and held without cause or indefinitely without being tried.

Exercise A: Indicate whether each of the following statements is true or false by writing the letter T or F in the space provided.

—1. Courts have been developed to interpret and to apply the law and to settle disputes arising between individuals and groups.

—2. Each court has one judge to see that its proceedings are carried out according to the law and to decide what evidence may be admitted.

—3. As officers of the court, attorneys are not expected to assist in determining the facts.

—4. Many courts have judge to keep their records.

—5. Such other officers as marshals, bailiffs, or sheriffs perform such duties as keeping order in court.

Exercise B: Do the court systems of Korea differ a little from those of America in the administration of justice?

Appendix

Business English for Jobs

Overview

Section 1	Vocabulary	Job skills and abilities
Section 2	Language Emphasis	Tense: Present perfect
Section 3	Reading Skills	Resumes
Section 4	Writing Skills	Resumes
Section 5	Language Emphasis 2	Tense: Past simple and present perfect
Section 6	Practice Skills	Job interview skills
Appendix		Supplementary vocabulary Exercise Answers Key

Warm up

Among the following jobs, which do you believe get paid the least and which do you believe get paid the most? Please create a list of these jobs in order from the highest salary to the least.

- Fast food cashier
- Doctor
- Software CEO
- Elementary school teacher
- Professional baseball player
- Lawyer
- Police officer

Are there any jobs you can think of that have extremely high salaries? What about low salaries?

In the list below, please either mark "yes" or "no" if you would like the following in your job.

___ frequent business trips

___ working in a large corporation
___ working with the same coworkers everyday
___ having your own office
___ sharing a cubicle with a coworker
___ talking on the phone frequently
___ working together as a team
___ working individually
___ working on the weekend
___ corporate attire or uniforms
___ casual attire, relaxed wear

When considering a job or career, do you value money or enjoyable work?

Section 1

Vocabulary– Job Skills and Abilities

In this section, you will learn some common business–related vocabulary focused upon job skills and abilities. Such vocabulary is often found in job listings, resumes, and job descriptions. Learning such vocabulary will give you an advantage in describing your own skill sets clearly as well as understanding the qualifications of a company's job opening.

Exercise A

From the list of words below, please use these words to fill in the blank from the job advertisement in Figure 1.

train(a) *supervise(b)* *increase(c)* *improve(d)*
organize(e) *communicate(f)*

Fig.
Job Advertisement #1337
Position: Director, Product Management
Company: Namba Marketing
Responsibilities:
1. Improve communication between our clients and marketing team. (make better)
2. ________ profit margins by 20% next quarter. (make more)
3. ________ new employees in using our marketing software. (instruct)
4. ________ our current database to make it more efficient. (put in order)
5. ________ with current clients to set up business meetings. (talk)
6. ________ a small team of assistant marketers. (take charge of)

Exercise B

Similar to exercise A, please use the words below to fill in the blank in Fig.2.

Interpret(a) *publish(b)* *develop(c)* *resolve(d)*

Fig.2
Job Advertisement #1337 –continued
Qualifications:
Currently, in your job you:
1.______ new programs to increase market share. (create)
2.______ conflicts between a client's and your company's interest. (work out)
3.______ between foreign clients and your company. (translate, explain)
4.______ articles current topics to increase your company's publicity. (write)

Exercise C

Please explain what skills and abilities which are required in your past or current jobs. Please use simple past tense or simple present tense in forming your answers. Only use the verbs from Exercises A and B.

Example:

In my past job I trained all of the new employees.

In my current job I resolve problems between coworkers.

Additional vocabulary

Management Skills	Communication Skills	Clerical Skills
administered	addressed	approved
analyzed	corresponded	catalogued
contracted	mediated	implemented
delegated	motivated	inspected
evaluated	promoted	monitored
produced	publicized	processed
reviewed	recruited	systematized
Research Skills	**Technical Skills**	**Teaching Skills**
collected	assembled	advised
diagnosed	computed	coordinated
evaluated	engineered	facilitated
examined	maintained	initiated
identified	overhauled	instructed
interviewed	programmed	persuaded
surveyed	upgraded	stimulated
Financial Skills	**Creative Skills**	**Helping Skills**
allocated	conceptualized	assessed
appraised	designed	assisted
audited	fashioned	counseled
budgeted	illustrated	educated
forecasted	invented	expedited
marketed	performed	rehabilitated
projected	revitalized	represented

Section 2

Language Emphasis – Present Perfect Tense

"I have slept"

The present perfect tense is an essential tense used in the English language, but oftentimes it can be challenging for non–native speakers. This is due to the fact that it uses conceptual ideas that do not exist in most languages. Even though the structure of the present perfect tense is very straightforward, the trouble lies with the use of the tense.

Structure:

Subject + auxiliary verb (**have**) + main verb (**past participle**)

Examples:

	subject	auxiliary verb		main verb	
+	I	have		seen	the movie.
+	You	have		studied	hard.
–	She	has	not	been	to Korea.
–	We	have	not	practiced	our song.
?	Have	you		eaten?	
?	Have	they		finished	yet?

Contractions with the present perfect tense:

Usually while speaking in present perfect tense, we use contractions between the subject and auxiliary verb. Also, during more informal writings we may use such contractions.

Tip:

He's or **she's**??? The ('s) contraction is used for the verbs "have" and "be". A tricky example is, "It's eaten" which can mean:

- It **has** eaten. [present perfect tense, active voice]
- It **is** eaten. [present tense, passive voice]
  Usage
- We use the present perfect tense to talk about actions that continue from the past into the present.

I have	I've
You have	You've
He has She has It has Jenny has The table has	He's She's It's Jenny's The table's
We have	We've
They have	They'e

I **have lived** in Seoul for 9 years. (Presently, I am still living in Seoul.)

She **has worked** for this firm for 25 years. (Presently, she is still working for this firm)

- Oftentimes, the present perfect tense can be used to talk about job experiences.

  He **has had** 2 corporate jobs since graduating from SKKU.

  She **hasn't had** any job related work experience since leaving his first company.

  Have you ever **worked** in accounting? Yes, I **have.** / No, I **haven't.**

Exercise D

In this exercise, please match the job interview questions on the left with their corresponding answers on the right.

1) How many jobs have you had since graduating?	a) Yes, I have won two academic scholarships as well as an award in my research.
2) Have you ever worked for a company that you didn't like?	b) I wanted more responsibility and a higher salary.
3) In what ways has your position changed over the course of your career?	c) I've worked for 3 different firms.
4) Why have you changed jobs so frequently?	d) In the beginning, I started off as an assistant, but now I have worked as a manager for the past 12 years.
5) Have you earned any accolades or awards in your career?	e) My last company was very difficult to work for.

Exercise E

Below is a list of interview questions. Please fill in the blanks while using the present perfect form of the verbs highlighted in brackets.

1) What ____________ [you learn] from your previous jobs?
2) What ____________ [you do] that shows your management and leadership skills?
3) Can you describe the types of coworkers ____________ [you work] with?
4) What other companies ____________ [you send] an application to?
5) What computer applications ____________ [you use] in your past jobs?
6) What conflicts or problems ____________ [you solve] in your past jobs?
7) How ____________ [you grow] over the last 5 years?
8) What kinds of projects ____________ [you supervise] in the past?
9) What ____________ [you read] recently in the newspapers?

10) Why __________ [you apply] for this job?

Exercise F

Find a partner and work in pairs for this exercise. Pick one person to ask the interview questions in Exercise E, while the other person answers. After completing each question, switch roles and repeat.

Section 3

Reading Skills- Resume

First Impressions

The resume or curriculum vitae is the most important document when seeking employment in the business world. The resume is essentially the first meeting between you and a prospective employer. In other words, it is the first impression you will make. So, how do you want to be remembered? Messy and chaotic. Clean and organized. Long and dull. Defined and fascinating. Oftentimes, there are such large influxes of applicants that companies do not have enough time to meet them all for interviews. So, companies enlist an eliminating process- resumes.

Informative

Resumes contain a wealth of information and tell an employer a lot about you. It contains your entire professional and academic history along with your growth and potential. However, herein lies the catch as you must convince the employer within moments of reading your resume that you deserve further attention before it is discarded. Resumes need to be clear, succinct, and professionally organized. When writing a resume, your aim is to invoke an immediate reaction from the reader that says, "I am a perfect candidate for this job and you want to hire me". In this case, it is important to cater your resume differently for each separate job you're applying to.

Goal

The ultimate goal of writing a resume is to get called in for an interview. As stated above, you want an employer to read your resume and be eager to want to know more about you. Thus, a good resume will by your key to success, while a poorly written resume can result in a lost opportunity. A good resume will emphasize your strengths while de-emphasizing your weaknesses. Although it must be noted that you should never lie on a resume as it can result in costly consequences in the future. You want your resume to reflect yourself at your strongest and leave a strongly positive impression upon the reader.

Exercise G

From the list of words below, please use these heading titles to fill in the blank from the job resume in Figure 3.

Skills(a)   References(b)   Work Experience(c)   Interests(d)   Education(e)

Fig. 3

Name: Alek Bituin
Nationality: Filipino American
Address: 7158 1stAve
New York, NY 10028
Telephone: 1-707-437-1583
Email: akbituin@mail.com

_________*(1)*

2000-2004 Bachelor's of Arts in Managerial Economics, University of California Davis
1996-2000 Secondary School: Armijo High School, Fairfield, CA

_________*(2)*

2008-2009 Regional Branch Manager, PE Instruments, New York, NY

- set up new marketing office in Queens, NY
- trained the initial marketing team of 25
- developed new marketing strategies to increase sales

2004-2008 Sales Representative, FF Instruments, Fairfield, CA

- sold a wide range of products
- organized and presented potential clients with seminars

_________*(3)*

- Fluent in Tagalog, English, Spanish, and French
- Computer skills: Microsoft Word, Excel, PowerPoint, Photoshop, HTML

Interests(4)

- Hiking, travel, debate, bodybuilding

_________*(5)*

- Professional and personal references available on request.

Exercise H

By referencing Fig. 3 (sample resume), mark each following statement as true or false.

1)____ Alek Bituin studied in New York City

2)____ He is interested in staying physically fit

3)____ He has worked for three different companies

4)____ He has sold products in Fairfield, CA

5)____ He has organized seminars while working for PE Instruments

6)____ He has about 8 years of working experience

Exercise I

Work in pairs or groups of 3 to answer the following questions regarding the differences between resumes from the following examples and ones used in your country.

1) Are there any rules to how many pages a resume can be in your country?
2) Do you use the same types of headings as those within the above examples?
3) Do you have to include a photo? Is this a good or bad practice?
4) Does your country usually ask for any other information to include in your resume?

Additional examples of different styles of resumes used within the US Market:

CASEY LE JEUNE

843A Gotham Street · San Francisco, CA 94122 · (415) 424-6480 · caseylee@mail.com

PROFESSIONAL EXPERIENCE

ICN COMMERCE, San Francisco, CA August 2004 – Present

Associate (January 2006 – Present)

– Saved $2.5 million(25% cost reduction) for a global manufacturing company by managing the sourcing of facility services within a unionized environment

– Realized 3:1 ROI within one year by leading the design and implementation of a $3 billion buying center operation for a software technology firm

– Tracking over $500 thousand in annual profit by managing supplier transactions for a global retail company

Analyst (August 2004 – December 2005)

– Saved $2.2 million (16% cost reduction) for global retailer by supporting sourcing of direct materials and services

– Streamlined supplier relations by developing internal tracking tool for up to 500 suppliers currently used company-wide

– Rated top 5% in my Analyst pper group by my direct supervisors in formal year-end review

PARCH INSURANCE GROUP, San Francisco, CA May 2003 – August 2004

Executive Assurance Underwriter

– Assessed insurance premiums with up to $25 million in coverage for executives of private and public companies through financial statement analysis and liability risk foretasting

– Improved broker relations by effectively managing communication between 20 brokers across 5 brokerage firms

– Completed the one-year internal training program in only four months by taking additional insurance

VOLUNTEER EXPERIENCE

HANDS IN BAY AREA (HIBA), San Francisco, CA January 2005 – Present

Leadership Development Committee Member

– Spearheaded first "Project Leader Peer Power" conference for leadership development and support within HIBA

– Managed monthly recurring "Project Leader Peer Power" conference by securing location, updating the meeting agenda, and maintaining participant attendance targets

– Increased new Project Leaders by 17% in one month by leading multiple formal two–hour training presentations

EDUCATION

UNIVERSITY OF CALIFORNIA, BERKELEY
Bachelor of Arts in Economics and Minor in Business Administration
August 1999 – May 2003
GPA: 3.9

Aleksandr Bituin
205 Harrison St. #320
San Francisco, CA94105
Cell: (510) 708-0312
Email: alek_bituin@hotmail.com

Education
University of California, Berkeley(August1999–May2003)
Bachelor of Arts, Double Major – Molecular and Cell Biology (Genetics and Development);
Integrative Biology (Evolution)
Cumulative GPA: 3.3

Professional Experience
Navigant Consulting, Inc., SanMateo,CA(July2003-Present)
– Specialized independent consulting firm providing litigation, financial, restructuring, strategic and operational consulting services
Senior Consultant - Healthcare Practice (Life Sciences Group)
– Authored market reports on emerging trends in the life sciences industry, including siRNA technology, acne and rosacea therapeutics, and sleep disorders therapeutics

Professional Service Solutions, Inc., SanFrancisco,CA(December2003-June2003)
– Boutique firm providing strategy consulting and advisory services to senior executives in the healthcare industry.
Associate
– Evaluated the information, analytics and reporting capabilities of a large pharmaceutical company.
– Interviewed senior level clients to gain insight on their analytics and reporting needs.
– Performed financial analysis that pinpointed potential cost–savings areas
– Created high–level profiles of internal IT systems and OLAP tools
– Developed and presented strategic recommendations to senior level management
– Developed of methodology for comparative ROI analysis of promotional expenditures of pharmaceutical products
– Built financial model of currently marketed and soon–to–be launched injectable drugs to determine their effect on health plans
– Developed strategy for PSS business development activities and created proposal documents

Front Line Strategic Consulting, Inc., SanMateo,CA(July2003-December2003)
– Life sciences market research firm providing consulting services to senior level management
Analyst - Strategic Market Report Division
– Authored market reports analyzing emerging technology and therapeutic drugs in the biotechnology and pharmaceutical industry
– Developed, recruited and conducted surveys with industry and academic experts
– Created financial models based on internal databases (IMS Health, Adis),

company reports and industry interviews
– Presented and defended reports to clients and sales team management

Related Experience
Tularik, Inc., South San Francisco, CA(May2003-July2003)
Summer Intern – Tularik Pharmaceutical Company

Activities
OASES (Oakland Asian Student Educational Services), Oakland, CA(Jan.2001-Present)
Secretary, OCAC Board of Directors
– Currently Secretary of Alumni Club; formerly student coordinator that managed over 400 volunteer tutors

Interests – Volunteering with youth, Comedy screenwriting

Section 4

Writing Skills– Resume
Types of Resumes

As with any form of writing, it is inevitable that each separate work has its own style. A personal style of word choice and organization can affect a potential employer's reaction to your resume accordingly. It is acceptable to take certain liberties when writing your resume, but all resumes should conform to a few certain rules.

The **chronological resume** is the most common form. It's a chronological listing of your job experience and other related experience with the most recent mentioned first. It is best for:

- People who have applicable work experience without many gaps in employment and minimal job changes
- People who have a linear job career history in a single profession

Its categories usually include at a minimum:

- Contact Information
- Objective
- Skills
- Work experience
- Education

The **functional resume** is less common, but can be equally if not more effective.

This type of resume emphasizes your skills and accomplishments more than the timeline of when you developed them. It is best for:

- People who have changed jobs a lot, but have lots of related experience.
- People who have no previous professional work experience. (entry level)
- People who are returning to the workforce after a long hiatus
- People who are trying to change career paths and want to highlight their skills and credentials
- People who have had little to none career growth.
- Military personnel who are trying to enter the civilian workforce

Its categories usually include if applicable:

- Contact Information
- Objective (optional)
- Work experience
- Volunteer experience

- Skills
- Education
- Affiliations
- Licenses
- Publications / Patents
- Honors or Awards

General rules and practices

Following these general rules and practices will keep your resume clean, well organized, and effective in catching and keeping your potential employer's eye.

- Keep your resume at one (1) page max, unless you have extensive work experience.
- Always include the month/year to all experiences, jobs, and activities.
- Use strong action verbs. (Use the table in the earlier vocabulary section)
- Employers react better to numbers and figures rather than lengthy explanations of accomplishments
- Avoid the use of "I" as a subject.
- Don't include ALL of your experiences, but rather focus on the most transferable (skills that are similar) to the job you are applying for.
- Do not decorate your resume or use decorative typefaces
- Use a professional email address (example:jthiraga@mail.com vs. SpeedRacerBoy@import-racer.com)
- Pay attention to the general composition of your resume. There should be a balance between the "black" and "white" spaces on your resume.
- Proofread. Proofread. Proofread.

Things to never include in your resume

When employers receive resumes, they can be quite unforgiving when making a judgment about resumes. Spelling mistakes or any of the following can lead to a direct path from your resume to the trash bin. Things never to include in your resume:

- **A resume title**
  ▷ It should be obvious that this is your resume
- **Availability**
  ▷ It should be obvious that you are available. If you are not, you should not be sending out your resume until you are.
- **Salary**
  ▷ If your request is too high, you can be rejected immediately and if it is too low, you may pay you what you asked for even if it is less than what they were preparing to pay.

- **Mention of Age, Race, Religion, Sex, or National Origin**

▷ This applies only if you are applying for a US company. There are laws that explicitly prohibit discrimination and many employers are "Equal Opportunity Employers" (EOE), which makes this information useless. Instead, use this extra space on your resume to reinforce your qualifications.

- **Photographs**

▷ This applies only if you are applying for a US company. Again, this has to do with discrimination laws and if unnecessary to attach to your resume.

- **Charts and Graphs**

▷ You really shouldn't have that much free space to put such a graphic in. If you do, fix it. Charts and graphs are unacceptable.

- **Weaknesses**

▷ It is counter-productive. You should be focusing on emphasizing your strengths and not your weaknesses.

- **Reasons for Leaving**

▷ In describing your previous job positions, it is inappropriate to put this information in your resume. If the employer wants to know your reasons for leaving, he or she will ask you directly.

- **References**

▷ It is unprofessional to list your references in your resume. Instead, you may choose to write "References are available upon request." at the end of your resume. Although, this practice is slowly dwindling as it is assumed nowadays that this is a given.

Exercise J

Fill out the contact information below:

a. Name:

b. Permanent address:

c. Phone number:

d. Email address:

Exercise K

An objective is a short 1-2 sentence section where you summarize the position you are applying for and your main qualifications and/or your professional goal. Write an objective for any job of your choice. Be as specific as you can.

Example: A position as a Support Specialist allowing me to use my skills in the fields of computer science and management information systems.

Example: An opportunity to obtain a loan officer position, with eventual advancement to vice president for lending services, in a growth–oriented bank.

Exercise L

Make a list of your current jobs, experiences, and skills. Write down as many as you can.

Exercise M

Next, choose your intended career and circle only those that are most transferable to the skills / qualifications necessary for performing well in your intended career. These will be your most important focus points in your resume.

Exercise N

By using the information provided in exercises 1–4, create your own resume for any job you wish. Review the guidelines and general rules before beginning. Furthermore, you may refer to the previous sample resumes for an example of how to format your resume.

Section 5

Language Emphasis 2 – Past Simple and Present Perfect Tense

"I slept" and "I have slept"

In Language Emphasis 1, the present perfect tense was covered, and so in this section we will focus on the past simple tense. We can use many different tenses to talk about the past, but the past simple tense is the most common.

Form:

Past form only

or

auxiliary **did** + **base form**

Examples of regular and irregular verbs:

	Base form	Past form	
Regular verb	work manage like	worked managed liked	The past form of regular verbs always end with –ed
Irregular verb	go see sing	went saw sang	The past form of irregular verbs is variable. You need to memorize these.

Structure:

Positive sentence: Subject + main verb (past form)

Negative sentence: Subject + auxiliary verb (did) + not + main verb (base)

Question: auxiliary verb (did) + subject + main verb (base)

Examples:

	subject	auxiliary verb		main verb	
+	I			**went**	to work.
+	You			**studied**	very much.
–	She	**did**	not	**go**	to SNU.
–	We	**did**	not	**practice**	our lecture.
?	**Did**	you		**eat**	yet?
?	**Did**	they		**finish**	on time?

Exception for the verb "to be" is different. We conjugate the verb "to be" (I was, you were, he / she / it was, we were, they were); and do **not** use an auxiliary for question and negative sentences. Instead, to make a question, we exchange the subject and the verb.

	Subject	Main verb		
+	I, he / she / it You, we, they	was were		here. In Seoul.
−	I, he / she / it You, we / they	was were	not not	here. sad.
?	Was Were	I, he / she / it you, we, they		correct? early?

Usage

• We use the past simple tense to talk about completed actions that happened in the past.

I **lived** in Seoul for 8 years. (Presently, I live in another place.)

She **worked** for this firm for 1 year. (Presently, she works for another firm)

Exercise O

In this exercise, underline the past simple or the present perfect form of the verbs to correctly complete the following paragraph.

I believe I **had / have had** (1) an interesting career. I **studied / have studied** (2) at Stanford for my undergraduate degree from 1999–2003. I then **applied / have** applied (3) for jobs internationally around the world. Eventually, I **worked/ have worked** (4) in Korea for 3 years, and then I **went / have been** (5) to Thailand in 2007. I **lived / have lived** (6) in a variety of countries. I **sold/ have sold** (7) medical supplies in the United States. I **taught / have taught** (8) Marketing in Korea and still do. I **wrote / have written** (9) a textbook, and **ran / have run** (10) my own marketing firm which I still own today.

Exercise P

In the following exercise, circle the words or phrases that can be used to complete this sentence:

The president has been here ___________.

1) previously
2) right now
3) since 5:00pm
4) for six hours
5) recently
6) a couple years ago
7) at lunchtime
8) tomorrow
9) in a few hours
10) soon

Section 6

Practice Skills – Job Interview Skills

If you've submitted a well organized resume, you've probably received a call in for an interview. Congratulations, you've already passed the hard part in job hunting. Now that you've got the interview, you are already half way to getting that dream job. An interview signifies that you already possess the qualifications for this job and that the employers want to know more about you. At this point in the game, confidence, preparation, and clear communication are your keys to getting that job offer.

Exercise Q

In this exercise, work in pairs. Determine which of these interview tips are more geared toward candidates and which are more geared toward the interviewer.

a. Always arrive half an hour early for the interview.
b. Get a professional haircut.
c. Attempt to put the other party at ease.
d. Ask difficult questions early on in the interview.
e. Ask more open–ended questions vs. yes or no questions.
f. Take lots of notes and listen carefully.
g. Be entirely honest.
h. Be sure to be relax and but always keep yourself professional.

Exercise R

Work with a partner and determine which tips you agree with. Choose your top 3 tips and add 3 more of your own tips to your list. Compare your list with other groups. Are there any common tips that are seen as most important?

Exercise S

Roleplay. In this scenario, the manager of a marketing firm is interviewing a candidate for the job of Strategist. Work in pairs, one will lead the interview as the manager as the other answers the questions as the job candidate.

Note: candidate's answers are in the appendix

Marketing Manager: Find out this information about the job candidate.

1. Did / find / office okay?
2. Why / apply for this job?
3. What strengths / have?
4. What weakness / need to overcome?
5. Can / work under pressure?
6. What / learn from / last job?
7. What / not like about / last boss?
8. What / hobbies?
9. Do / have any questions?

Appendix

Supplementary vocabulary

accordingly - adv. therefore; so; in due course
agenda - n. a list, plan, outline, or the like, of things to be done
beforehand - adv. in anticipation; in advance; ahead of time
biotechnology - n. use of living organism to perform industrial or manufacturing process
brokerage - n. a firm who buys and sells stocks and bonds for clients
chaotic - adj. completely confused or disordered
chronological adj. - arranged in the order of time
conjugate - v. to join or inflect a verb
contraction - n. a work formed by omitting or combining some of the sounds
corporate ladder - n. the order of position, title, or rank, as in a large corporation
corporate attire - n. formal dress as is common in a large professional corporation
cubicle - n. a small space or compartment, oftentimes your own personal workspace
invoke - v. to call for
I.T. - n. an abbreviation for Internet Technology
liability - n. moneys owed; debts or obligations.
litigation - n. to contest or engage in legal proceedings.
max - adj. a common abbreviation for the word "maximum" (most)
messy - adj. characterized by dirty, untidy, or disordered
methodology - n. a set or system of methods and rules for regulating a given discipline
oftentimes - adv. often
ROI - n. a common abbreviation for 'return on investment'
sourcing - n. buying of components of a product from an outside supplier
straight forward - adj. going or directed straight ahead, direct
succinct - adj. expressed in a few words; concise; terse
tailored- adj. fitted for, custom made
therapeutic - adj. of pertaining to the treating or curing of disease; curative
ultimate - adj. last; furthest or farthest; highest
underwrite - v. to show agreement with by signing one' s name to a statement
unforgiving - adj. not allowing for mistakes or showing no mercy
unionize - v. to organize into a labor union

Answers to Exercises

Section 1

Exercise A	1.d, 2.c, 3.a, 4.e, 5.f, 6.b
Exercise B	1.c, 2.d, 3.a, 4.b

Section 2

Exercise D	1.c, 2.e, 3.d, 4.b, 5.a

Exercise E

Have you learned
Have you done
You have worked
Have you sent
Have you used
Have you solved
Have you grown
Have you supervised
Have you read
Have you applied

Section 3

Exercise G	1.e, 2.c, 3.a, 4.d, 5.b
Exercise H	1.T, 2.T, 3.F, 4.T, 5.F, 6.F

Section 5

Exercise O

Have had	Studied
Applied	Worked
Went	Have lived
Sold	Have taught
Wrote	Have run

Exercise P

Phrases that CAN complete the sentence: 1,3,4,5,6,7

Exercise S

Candidate for Strategist position
Answer the questions using this information.

1. Yes / came by train.
2. Enjoy working with big brands / want to work in NYC
3. Creative / fluent in English
4. Sometimes / work too hard
5. Very calm person
6. Excel / work with others
7. Poor communication
8. Film, hiking
9. Benefits / hours / typical day